ENLIGHTENMENT BEYOND TRADITIONS

ENLIGHTENMENT
BEYOND
TRADITIONS

AZIZ KRISTOF
HOUMAN EMAMI

MOTILAL BANARSIDASS PUBLISHERS
PRIVATE LIMITED ● DELHI

First Edition: Delhi, 1999

© AUTHOR
All Rights Reserved.

ISBN: 81-208-1651-x (Cloth)
ISBN: 81-208-1652-8 (Paper)

Also available at:

MOTILAL BANARSIDASS
41 U.A. Bungalow Road, Jawahar Nagar, Delhi 110 007
8, Mahalaxmi Chamber, Warden Road, Mumbai 400 026
120 Royapettah High Road, Mylapore, Chennai 600 004
Sanas Plaza, 1302, Baji Rao Road, Pune 411 002
16 St. Mark's Road, Bangalore 560 001
8 Camac Street, Calcutta 700 017
Ashok Rajpath, Patna 800 004
Chowk, Varanasi 221 001

PRINTED IN INDIA
BY JAINENDRA PRAKASH JAIN AT SHRI JAINENDRA PRESS,
A-45 NARAINA, PHASE I, NEW DELHI 110 028
AND PUBLISHED BY NARENDRA PRAKASH JAIN FOR
MOTILAL BANARSIDASS PUBLISHERS PRIVATE LIMITED,
BUNGALOW ROAD, DELHI 110 007

This book is dedicated to the invisible intelligence-grace that had awakened the first human being to the absolute state, state of heart and beyond.... Thus initiating the very existence of the enlightenment in the consciousness of mankind.

To this force we bow in respect and gratitude for its unconditional love and guidance. May its universal presence bless the earthly existence of all who seek its wisdom within their own presence.

Contents

TRANSMISSION
FROM THE DIMENSION OF
UNDERSTANDING

Introduction

This Book is manifestation of the same Spirit that has allowed the human intelligence from the very beginning to reach the light of Understanding. This Spirit does not negate that which has been attained, as spiritual traditions, but embraces and transcends them as a part of its <u>own</u> past evolution. The mind wants to freeze the past spiritual conclusions as the ultimate, but the Spirit cannot stop in its eternal journey of expansion; for that would be against its very essence: Freedom.

Now the human collective consciousness has reached a very profound understanding of the Ultimate Reality. This understanding is present in a few of the great spiritual schools of Enlightenment. These traditions, having been created a few thousands years ago, have been evolving continuously until our time. However, their evolution so far cannot go beyond certain philosophical understandings that had been founded in their times, based on their given circumstances. Our attempt is to bring an understanding relevant to the current stage of spiritual evolution that can allow us to expand fully into the Universal Wholeness. For that reason, with the full respect and gratitude to the past traditions, we present in this book a Revelation of the New dimension of Awakening and Understanding.

The past traditions perceived only one dimension of growth: the expansion into the Inner State. Returning to the state of the original "white light" has been the highest ideal, resulting in the negation of other

dimensions of growth. Since the return to the Original
State is the purpose of growth in their vision, naturally
there is no place for the positive evolution into the all-
inclusive wholeness of <u>Me</u>. However, the awakening to
Me, which is the Soul, is our primal task. The Rainbow
that is an expression of the same original white light can
be manifested only when the Inner is completed and
transcended in a total acknowledgment and appreciation
of the very presence of Me.

The Revelation from the Beyond

Beyond the collective consciousness of humanity there is the all-embracing ocean of Universal Intelligence. Our evolution, taking place within the limitations of human intelligence, in order to reach the Realm of Wholeness, must transcend the frontiers of its own past. The human dimension, which is the divine limitation, merely represents a stage of growth of the Spirit in its expansion towards the Supreme Understanding. The human traditions, that is, the Past, are the ultimate limitation of our Now. The past giving birth to our present intelligence, has brought us to the point where no further expansion is possible. This is where the Revelation from the Beyond needs to enter. And it enters Unexpectedly. Grace is the hand of the Universal Intelligence that is leading its own past towards the Ultimate Fulfillment, which is the Supreme Now. It enters when evolution cannot free itself from its own past, and brings the liberating Light of the New. The quantum leap into the higher Understanding, freed from the past, cannot be done; it has got to be Revealed. And it is being Revealed.

The Vision of This Book

This book is not merely a description of the Supreme Understanding. Each chapter represents a certain important stage of human evolution towards a more and more complete understanding of the Reality. It is a continuous transcendence of what has been attained. Every chapter is a piece of truth, an angle of seeing the picture of reality. We are, in a non-linear way, reaching higher and higher understanding, coming closer to the final moment when our intelligence and the Reality merge into one. Moving within the shores of traditional teachings and using their highest attainments, we continuously test them with the fire of our intelligence. We remove and transcend those elements of past understanding that might obscure our growth and prevent us from reaching the Complete Understanding.

The simple purpose of this book is to show clearly the journey of consciousness from ignorance and confusion towards the full realization of the "I Am." The I Am we speak about is not merely what traditionally is called "no-mind," "presence" or "witnessing consciousness." These are just aspects of the I Am. The complete I Am is a unity of Enlightened Awareness, Enlightened Heart and Enlightened Rest upon the Absolute. However, it is not merely the realization of the I Am that is our ultimate goal, but the Enlightenment to "Me."

The reality of Me is even more mysterious than all the exalted inner states. Me is not given, but must be given birth to. The realization of the inner states allows finally the complete seeing of what Me is. The awakening of the inner states is not a final goal but a foundation upon which the real goal can be attained. This goal is the complete awakening to the dimension of Me. Though it is beyond states, Me rests upon them. The Final Enlightenment transcends the Inner, as well as the outer in the pure, transparent, absolutely direct, personal and intimate apperception of what "I Am." Enlightenment to Me is the real purpose of our evolution. We are here to discover fully and doubtlessly what Me is. Me, the experiencer and enjoyer of all states, finally must be awakened to itself. This is the highest beauty and the greatest joy; going beyond the illusion of spirituality, one at last discovers Oneself.

The Map of Awakening

I. IGNORANCE

Ignorance is a valid dimension, for it constitutes the experience of most human beings. Ignorance is an experience of oneself in which Me is completely fragmented, unconscious and without any center or foundation. The mechanical mind totally overpowers the psyche, not allowing one to experience either the Being or the Heart. In this state, one is totally identified with psychological events, thoughts and emotions. Because there is no center, every thought and emotion creates a separate Me, an identified Me. As in a dream, one lives in a fully objectified reality or one is this objectified reality, without the existence of a subject. Me is objectified and identified with what is perceived and thought. For that reason, one experiences suffering and negativity to a much higher degree.

The state of ignorance represents a very flat and narrow reality. There is no depth to it. The functions of awareness and sensitivity are very limited and unconscious in this state. In this state the Soul suffers, and at the same time is not aware of itself. The unconscious reigns. One lives in the world of ego-images; how one perceives oneself always relates to the outer. Ignorance cannot be regarded as a conscious state. It is between the conscious and the unconscious. It is vague, unclear and empty of any real substance. It is to be transcended. This is the challenge, sooner or later, of every human being.

II. AWAKENING OF THE I AM

"I Am" is the full experience of oneself prior to the movement of thoughts and emotions. This experience is a unity of Awareness, energy of Being and the Heart. All these aspects need to be integrated within oneself to manifest the Wholeness.

Attention

In order to transcend the mind we must first awaken the aspect of Attention, the seed of being conscious within the mind. This attention is generated in the mind, and due to it, the unconscious, mechanical aspect of the very mind becomes transcended. The self-recognizing attention, when seen in itself as separated from the "perceived," gives rise to the state of Presence. The purpose of the cultivation of attention is integration of and stabilization in the Presence, so that it finally becomes a constant and stable center of awareness at the background of the psychological self. However, if other aspects of "I Am" are not developed, and the Presence is cultivated alone, one can become very imbalanced.

Being

The Being aspect is what gives to the Presence the necessary depth. The Presence without Being is too intense and deprived of the quality of rest, relaxation and letting go. Cultivating the Being aspect allows the energy of Presence to be dropped and pulled by the natural gravitational force, downward throughout the whole body. First, one lets go of the mind by shifting the attention to the Presence. Next, one relaxes the will of self-referring Presence which will gently dissolve into the state of non-doing, effortless sitting and pure meditation.

Naturally, in activity the Attention aspect is more exposed, while in sitting meditation, the Being aspect is. At this point, the Attention and Being aspect of the I Am are present.

Heart
Without bringing into the state of Being and Attention the quality of deep sensitivity of the awakened Heart, one is far from experiencing the complete I Am. Although we describe the Heart as the center of feeling, at the same time it is a dimension of Being. The energetic presence of the Heart brings warmth to the coolness of awareness and being. Heart is the balance between the inner and the outer, without which one is pulled in too much, and the relationship with the outer cannot be harmonious and expansive. We are essentially feeling beings, and the intimate center of our identity as "Me" is placed in the Heart. Without the Heart we cannot experience fundamental sensitivity and inner beauty. Developing the attention and working simultaneously with the other two aspects, we come closer and closer to the holistic experience of the I Am. Only when all of these aspects are integrated, do we feel fulfilled and happy.

III. THE ABSOLUTE STATE

Beneath the I Am is a place of Absolute Rest. The Absolute is a secret of the Being aspect of the I Am. The Awareness or Heart cannot reach the Absolute. The complete surrender happens only through the Being. Prior to the shift to the Absolute, the experience of being belongs to the I Am. We can say it is a part of Me, as if the energy of being couldn't go beyond its frame of reference. For that reason, the Being aspect of the I

Am which is responsible for the experience of peace and rest, cannot reach the Absolute Rest. The peace and rest experienced within the I Am has a quality of a certain movement of energy and consciousness. It is beautiful, and for most souls, the ultimate. However, there is a deeper experience that goes beyond the I Am.

The shift to the Absolute expands the Being aspect of the I Am to its original absence, to the realm prior to consciousness and energy. The center of identity within the Being aspect is pulled to the Source itself, so one is in a very mysterious way placed prior to the I Am. Here, the state of Pure Rest is manifested. The Being aspect of the I Am can completely let go of itself, and be received by the Unborn. It is here that Me can finally experience its own absence within the presence of the universal I AM.

IV. FINAL ENLIGHTENMENT: TO ME

The "Me" that entered the spiritual path and is completing all of the inner states, is still in a mysterious way, unconscious of itself. One can be Enlightened to the I Am and to the Absolute, and still be unaware of the very Me who has reached Enlightenment. Who is the seeker? Who is the finder? It is here that a totally new understanding beyond the knowledge of traditions emerges: awakening to Me. But without the realization of the inner states, one is not capable of seeing what this Me truly is. The inner states create the perfect environment, a spotless mirror in which the Me at last can be reflected and apperceived.

Without awakening to the Heart, Me cannot be seen as anything in particular. The center, the essence of Me, is in the Heart. We call it the Soul. Only in the heart can Me fully meet itself. However, first the foundation of the inner silence, depth of being and clarity of awareness are absolutely necessary. When the Heart is awakened, it no longer remains in the middle of our chest but becomes the totality of our being.

What is Me? It is the wholeness of what I am which is absolutely personal and intimate. It is the oneness of Presence, stillness of Being, warmth and sensitivity of the Heart and the movement of Intelligence. When the Me is awakened to itself, it no longer rests in the "other" states, but in itself. In effortless abiding, it becomes one with the universal I AM, and meets the Creator.

Enlightenment to "Me," which is the flowering of the Soul or individual evolution, reaches through itself, its ultimate expansion. It merges into the apperception of that which is beyond its ultimate frontiers, the Universal I AM. Here, the individual Me transcends itself into the Supreme Dimension beyond Unity and Separation.

I

Realm of the Inner

1

Realm of the Inner

Toward the Presence

Waking up from the dream of unconsciousness is a painful and complicated process. Our desire is to show how the personal and spiritual dimensions correlate and constitute each other; to show how the process of spiritual realization unfolds. The personality is seen not as an obstacle in this process, but rather as an indivisible and integral part of the path towards the Unmanifested. Later we will return to the personality itself, as it fulfills its own purpose in the manifestation (apart from spiritual fulfillment) while simultaneously being witnessed by the original state.

TOWARD THE SELF

How could a person, being fully identified with the functioning of his/her mind, be able to turn the light back from becoming, toward being? Be-coming is a never-ending, never satisfied movement of *coming* to *be*. Becoming can never *come* to *be* because it is not able to rest. Becoming doesn't know what rest is. Becoming is time, and time is manifestation. Manifestation is the becoming. In the search for the state of Being, we express our longing to find in existence a place beyond becoming. From a certain perspective, we are the prisoners of time; we have no way to escape—for we *are* time itself.

What is Being? The original state only *is;* there is no element of time in it. Being is the place where the manifested meets its Source. This meeting creates a new quality which is beyond becoming and beyond the isness of the Absolute. This new quality is called Be-ing. Being is a state of resting, that is, being unmoved. It is occurring in time, but is not from time. Being is a state in which the becoming, which is time, becomes one with its timeless origin, giving rise to the state of Rest.

THE PATH

When the aspiration of going beyond the illusion arises— it is time to enter the precious Path. The inner call has been heard, but how to respond to it? Which direction to go? How shall one begin?

Meditation and Inquiry: The two most significant elements of our journey. Meditation is the art of entering our inner reality directly. Inquiry relates to the very important use of certain intuitive faculties of our intellect which accelerate the process of growth and give us a tool to discern the real from illusion. We can look at them as separate, but in reality they are deeply interconnected. Meditation develops concentration, mindfulness and samadhi, but without inquiry there would be no understanding or wisdom.

On the deeper level are two essential qualities of that which we are: Being and Understanding. Being without Understanding is dull and passive. Understanding without Being is agitated, restless and devoid of basic calm and stillness. Meditation must be supported by inquiry, while inquiry without meditation is meaningless and intellectual.

A one sided attitude is quite common. Inquiry without meditation is a very limited approach. One accumulates a lot of spiritual information, gets to know many masters and has plenty of conceptual answers relating to spiritual matters without going into actual practice. One truly does not reach any state; on the contrary–one becomes more and more disconnected from the realm of silence.

Meditation without inquiry is also a very common approach among those who are not somehow intellectually sensitive to the dimension of Being. Usually they take for granted all the one-sided views claiming meditation is "not-thinking," and by following them, they block the *natural* inquiring mind. Many Zen students fall under this category. They prefer to think about some abstruse Zen saying or interview's answer, than to contemplate directly their own mind.

Meditation is not simply "not-thinking." It is beyond thinking, and beyond thinking includes thinking and not-thinking. To sit in meditation is to be in a state of consciousness which is naturally deeper than the occurrence of thoughts. Thinking does not decrease its depth nor does not-thinking increase it. Meditation is "non-doing" in which we let go of our relative consciousness. But although it is *non-doing*, it must still be attained.

There is "meditation" and "reaching meditation." It is a goal to be attained, the path to this goal and the presence of a complete state, all at the same time. In the process of arriving at the pure meditation state (Shikan-taza), the goal is already secretly present, and presents itself from time to time as a part of the meditator's experience. The further we go, the more our goal and the path become unified–until the path dissolves into the goal.

Before we go further into the deeper levels of meditation, let's say something about the beginning of the path. We need to remember that the maturity of practice cannot be measured by time--state of consciousness is the only criteria.

A person who doesn't have any background and has just entered the Path knows only thinking. In this mind, which knows only thinking, suddenly arises the aspiration to go beyond thinking. How can it be done? Interesting problem, isn't it? Where can we find a secret door to slip beyond thinking? One can anesthetize the mind with mantras or concentration techniques, but certainly that will not lead us beyond thinking. To go beyond thinking one needs be extremely alert and not merely hypnotized by artificial semi-meditative techniques.

Because we are unconscious, our attention is constantly being lost in the arising of thoughts. We have become those thoughts. Who are we apart from thoughts? Thoughts are our life. We think not only about our life--we actually think our life! No wonder that our thoughts are so dear to us. Thinking unfortunately has become very mechanical and to a great extent—obsessive. We think so much about our security and happiness, that this very thinking deprives us from basic peace and sanity.

When a thought pops up, our conscious or rather semi-conscious mind gets involved automatically and a new stream of thoughts spins us around. There seems to be no end to this. Fortunately the mind has a very precious ability of creating from time to time a self-conscious impulse, in which it refers to itself as being conscious of its immediate past. This is a moment when we realize that we have just been thinking. For example we are daydreaming, as it often happens, and suddenly something brings us to the present moment—like a click—our involvement stops and we are at the zero point. We also use exactly the same mechanism, as a passage from our mechanical mind to awareness. Our task is to transform this self-conscious impulse into a continuous momentum of attention.

In meditation we are using the self-conscious impulse as a tool to bring ourselves back to the present moment— to undo our habitual involvement in thinking. We try to see ourselves thinking and come as quickly as possible to the empirical reality, in which we feel ourselves sitting and are present to our surroundings. Because the mind is self-conscious only for a split second, noticing its past involvement in thoughts while simultaneously falling into the next thought, it is called an "impulse." The mind is still not self-conscious, but it has many self-conscious impulses.

The present moment is experienced here in a very vague way, as referring to objectivity. The mind cannot be self-conscious yet, for it simply is not able to embrace the self-conscious impulse *in itself*, that is, to be in it. We can call this touch of self-conscious impulse "being in the moment." This kind of "being in the moment" doesn't have the quality of Presence yet. Rather it is about being in empirical time (as opposed to mental time). Here, the flow of time from the immediate past into the present and the next moment, is identified by a subtle memory, as one experience.

When the mind learns how to recreate this self-conscious impulse as often as possible, we live more and more in empirical reality. The self-conscious impulse brings us back not only from our narrative thinking, but also from our involvement in empirical reality, which allows us to rearrange our attitude concerning what is happening around us.

Although the self-conscious impulse connects us with the present moment, the Non-doing or Shikan-taza is still much deeper. We need to investigate and dive into the *zero* point, where the self-conscious impulse does not fall into objectiveness but retains the precious stop and stays *in itself.* The moment the self-conscious impulse is able to experience itself as a continuity, the primal point of consciousness becomes awakened. This is the Presence itself..It is the moment when mindfulness refers to <u>itself</u> instead of the object.

Learning how to let go of thoughts from moment to moment, and the continuous re-awakening of the presence *here and now,* is basically all we do. The disciplined and proper meditation posture is very helpful to develop mindfulness. In the beginning, when the mind is excessively restless, we might calm it down with awareness of breath. Awareness of breath is a very natural way of connecting with empirical time, the present moment. It affects the mind directly and has a very strong healing and calming impact on our emotional body. Breathing slowly in the belly is very important to balance the energy and to accelerate the process of stabilization in the Presence.

We should not rely too much on any technique but learn how to sit without any kind of support—in the state of *non-doing.* It is very important to keep the balance of alertness and calmness; we need to be absolutely alert in the vivid, bright space of mindfulness. In this way, we dissolve unconsciousness and increase the continuity of being present. On the other hand, the calmness deepens the alertness and integrates it with non-doing; and by resting in the calmness, the alertness can become effortless and natural as well. Calmness without alertness becomes dull and passive without the power to further accelerate the development of our meditation.

It is very difficult to pin point what actually happens in this shift from the artificial, restless levels of the mind to the profound condition of Being. We are not merely tranquilizing the mind—there is an actual change of dimensions. We can speak about the forth dimension of consciousness. We normally live in a very flat reality; there is no depth because the *seer* is not present to itself. It is only the awakening of the witness-presence that can expand our three dimensional perception into a panoramic awareness. Mind is a movement that has got to perpetuate its continuity. That's why remaining in the state of non-abiding without support is against its habitual tendencies. But thanks to our practice, the mind expands into its deeper layers, and the movement gradually subsides into the stillness.

When the terms "mind" and "no-mind" are used, we tend to believe that they are separated. This creates difficulties in understanding the whole process of reaching the no-mind from the perspective of the mind. One wants to eliminate the mind in order to attain the no-mind. This is a big misunderstanding. First of all, it is through the mind that we reach the no-mind in a conscious way. Second, after we reach it, we see clearly that the mind is a natural extension of our own Presence. The original no-mind is not aware. It is through consciousness that we can reach the no mind, that is—to <u>become conscious</u> of it. To be conscious of no-mind does not mean that it becomes an *object* of consciousness. Consciousness without content is what we call "no-mind." The mind expands into its own nature. It awakens to that which is inherent in it, although not fully actualized yet.

We are part of the evolution of consciousness—an evolution that is conscious. It is no longer purely biological and instinctive. Our ego-mind is inquiring into itself using its will, intelligence, sensitivity and intention. In meditation, the mind learns how to rest in its nature which is *stillness,* and through inquiry we awaken the conscious link between our manifested mind and its essential core-nature.

We have already mentioned inquiry. In some mysterious way, the part of us that *understands* is absolutely indivisible from the process of meditation. Inquiry is not simply "thinking about" or conceptualizing. It belongs to the very intuitive part of our intellect. Understanding takes place when the experience or *being the experience* and intellectual insight, intuitively become one. In our spiritual inquiry we use ideas and concepts in a very skillful way—as if applying them and letting go of them at the same time. While inquiring, we are *being* with our state and *looking at* it simultaneously. In this looking, there is *nobody* who is looking, neither is it just a "choiceless awareness"—there is a profound desire to understand. In inquiry, the understanding can not be reached—it must be revealed! We allow the understanding manifest itself. Even so, we are not merely passive; in a very subtle and *empathetic* way, our intellectual sensitivity triggers the *knowing* to present itself. This is very significant, for it shows us how the mind-ego, from its layers of deep sensitivity, participates in the process of shifting to the dimension of the no-mind.

Who am I? Continuing the issue of inquiry, we would like to shed a little light upon one of the most fundamental inquiring questions. The question "Who am I?" is the essence of the whole journey of human spiritual evolution. It is through this question that ignorance finally begins to know itself as ignorance. We need a great deal of spiritual sensitivity to become aware of the fact that we really do not know who we are. The question, "Who am I?" brings an essential doubt into our old identification with the personality. But doubt is not enough. The desire to resolve it is essential. Without this overwhelming longing to *find out*, we will not be able to come out of the darkness.

There are many ways of approaching the question "Who am I?" On the superficial level, we might just give ourselves some new pseudo-spiritual labels like "soul" and "light" or pick up, for example, the Buddhist concept of "no-self," being convinced that we have solved the problem. But this is very naive for one cannot solve this riddle remaining on the level of concepts. The technique used in Advaita Vedanta approach goes much deeper. With this method, we take initially an assumption that what we really are is "eternal," "constant," "unchanging," and intellectually we eliminate all that doesn't fulfill these criteria. We contemplate: "I am not the body, I am not the mind—who am I really? What is there that remains?" This kind of inquiry combines the answer-seeking mind with a deep trust-knowing that what we are looking for is already present. In this way, the inquiry is happening *now*, refers to the now and finally, as the answer—becomes the Now.

The deepest meaning of the question "Who am I?" is even more subtle. It goes beyond the inquiry itself. The moment we want to find any resolution, the mind moves—it gets directed somewhere. But that which we truly are cannot be found in any direction; it is directionless. That's why the attempt to find oneself as being *something* or *somewhere* is already a mistake. It is like looking for one's head, wherever we look we miss the point. The seeker is the sought. The deepest purpose of our question is not to get to some place or to promote a doubt, but to create inside of our being a profound *stop*, which is the zero point of our consciousness. Our being knows. The knowledge of our true identity is already mysteriously present. What we need to do is to stop–<u>stop in it</u>.

CULTIVATION

Cultivation is not separated from the Path but it is beyond the gross level of seeking. We have previously mentioned that the Goal is mysteriously present at all times during the process of practice. Nevertheless, cultivation begins when the goal is clearly recognized. Unless we know who we are, unless we clearly recognize the state of Presence, we are more or less groping in the darkness. When the goal is finally clear, the real meditation begins. Consciousness is still not fully integrated with its essence, but the practice is no longer dualistic. This means that when mindfulness is present—its object (the Presence) is spontaneously present.

There are many views regarding how cultivation and Enlightenment relate. We need to remember that the term Enlightenment has two basic meanings. One is the recognition of the nature of the mind—an insight into the underlying state of Presence. The second is a state beyond cultivation. Usually when we speak about "Complete Enlightenment" we refer to the stage of realization in which cultivation doesn't apply any longer. In Zen for example, sometimes we find statements about the non-ending cultivation. Some masters propagate an opinion that one has got to practice zazen as long as one is alive. Is that really so? Well, we do not mind sitting zazen for pleasure, but the Enlightened person is certainly beyond practice. Some traditions really get addicted to practice. They don't seem to have full clarity about the proper relationship between cultivation and the final state of Self-realization. However, we would like to make clear that the stage "beyond cultivation" certainly does exist.

Another extreme view assumes that seeing into one's

Nature equals the end of cultivation. Usually those operating in an idealistic-linear logic propagate this kind of view. According to their view, either one sees the truth or not. There is no place for cultivation here. They don't seem to be in touch with the psychological reality of practice. The situation they describe is possible but occurs very, very rarely. It is called "sudden Enlightenment—sudden cultivation."

We should also mention that there are those who are able to recognize the essence of practice before entering the Path. In these cases, they start the Path with cultivation. We call this "sudden Enlightenment—gradual cultivation." But for most practitioners, the natural development consists of entering the Path, enhancing all those qualities which eventually promote the insight into the nature of Consciousness, cultivation and finally shifting beyond cultivation. The name for this is "gradual practice—gradual (or sudden) Enlightenment–gradual cultivation."

After the recognition of Presence, there is still a long way to go, but our practice is more and more positive. The practice is slowly turning into non-practice, where the cultivation unfolds naturally. Now we truly start to sit Shikan-taza, the non-doing. We finally are able to rest *beyond thinking* in the inner stillness.

In meditation, we can distinguish a few levels of consciousness. Witnessing Consciousness is the foundation and arising of gross thoughts occurs on the surface. In-between is something which we could call a movement of intuitive creative intelligence. This intuitive intelligence is in a dynamic relation with the arising of thoughts, as the material offered to it by the subconscious or as a reaction to its surroundings. It decides whether to let go of this information or to participate in it. This intuitive intelligence is also in a dynamic relation with the Witnessing Consciousness. For example, how it relates to the Presence is a direct cause of different levels of absorption in meditation. We could name this part of ourselves as the creative center of our personal intelligence.

When we speak about Witnessing Consciousness or "thoughtless awareness," we must remember that although it is *just present*, it is not at all static; it is a movement, the movement of silence-a fluctuation of consciousness itself. It is not enough to be aware of it. We need to get to know it—like a dear friend. We need to be with it, and in this "being"—learn. That's why an element of gentle inquiry absolutely needs to be present throughout the cultivation process. This intuitive intelligence can be delicately aware of the quality of the state of Presence without disturbing it. We can see how inner stillness and a subtle observing inquiry beautifully coexist as a harmonious whole. Neither the white clouds obscure the blue sky nor the deep blue sky hinders the floating clouds.

Let us say that however deep our meditation is, it is not enough, unless we truly understand ourselves. To understand ourselves we have to sit in the state of non-doing, while learning at the same time. This is not a contradiction, for as we already know, meditation is not just "not thinking" but *beyond thinking*. The state of Presence, though purely *now*, has many layers. It belongs to the vertical reality of the *now*, which some call the no-mind. But this *now* is multidimensional. The no-mind notion doesn't refer to some kind of static state, but to an alive and very rich organism of consciousness. It is not only *being*, it is *living*.

Consciousness has to be completely understood. We need to know it like our own garden. If we have a beautiful little garden in the countryside which we love very much and spend all of our spare time taking care of, we simply <u>know</u> it. Although it is always changing, all that you see there, the flowers, trees and plants, are always familiar and known. This is what is meant by understanding consciousness—it becomes embraced. One doesn't need to be highly accomplished to see that there are many different states of absorption. What this means is that consciousness, even while gross thinking is absent, can experience itself in various ways—it *tastes* differently. From the sharp and clear awareness in action it reaches deeper and deeper layers of calmness, going gradually into meditation, until it completely forgets itself and its surroundings in a trance-like Samadhi. There is no judgment about which of these states are more preferable. They are all valid as a part of the natural movement of consciousness; but it is necessary to comprehend them.

It is extremely important to realize that it is our intuitive intelligence that directly affects the quality of witnessing. It is this intelligence that decides whether it wants to be involved in the personal realm, or to rest in Being. When it is involved in the external reality or the mind, the witnessing is just passively present in the background. When it withdraws from the external reality, its energy naturally drops to the inner state and the witnessing goes deeper into itself.

In cultivation the understanding of consciousness is essential. But it is even more important to stabilize oneself firmly in the state of Presence. The presence of the goal needs to be constantly reawakened until finally it becomes our constant reality. Our effort gradually melts with the natural and spontaneous effortlessness of our being. cultivation turns into non-cultivation, and that which was our goal, transcends the path.

BEYOND CULTIVATION

The path and the goal have finally become one. The witnessing is effortless. No need to enhance one's practice any longer. But, as we have said, the dynamic relationship between the personality and Presence remains. This is a natural part of life. We have to face the constant challenge of recreating, throughout our life, this equilibrium between our involvement in the personal dimension and resting in the inner freedom. This balance is not automatically given for an awakened person, as some teachings might suggest. Although the spiritual and the mundane have become fully one—they are *two* at the same time. We must live this extraordinary paradox, for it represents Reality.

Going beyond cultivation means to be human again. Whatever our spiritual insight into the nature of reality is, being human is our destiny. With the completion of our cultivation the goal is forgotten. When the goal is forgotten, the naturalness is reached. When the naturalness is reached, our sensitivity and life become one.

This is not the end of the spiritual search. The Absolute has not been reached yet. Cultivation can not go beyond consciousness, for it belongs to this very consciousness. The understanding of the nature of consciousness takes place in the consciousness, but the longing to go beyond it comes from the Ultimate itself. The Ultimate is pure sensitivity; it is calling us and responds to our longing through Grace. There is no cultivation any more, only surrender. The surrender of the center of consciousness can not be done unless it encounters Grace. We know *what* needs to be surrendered but we do not know how and *to what*. In this not knowing the surrender consumes itself and implodes into Freedom. We can find no other word than Grace.

Toward the Unborn

This is the journey of Consciousness toward the realization of Ultimate Subjectivity from which everything has emerged and to which everything returns. This is a journey of the universe into itself, and through itself into the Beyond. All That Is, is but an expression of the Ultimate Subjectivity which experiences itself in its own objectivization. We need to understand that all that is occurring in the field of perception, that which is perceived, experienced and experienceable—all of it is but an expression of the Ultimate Subjectivity. Let's make no mistake: our spiritual journey is leading us beyond experience, which is itself the ultimate experience. That which we are is nothing but existence becoming self-conscious of itself as the manifested and waking up to its own absence, as its original identity. We, the manifested, are essentially that which is everlastingly unmanifested.

Consciousness is a tool with which the unmanifested translates itself into experience. It is in itself, the manifested reality. Consciousness is the *way* in which the manifested is recognized as manifested, but at the same time the only tool through which the unmanifested can be reached and recognized. The essence of consciousness is consciousness in itself, emptied from its content. We call it the state of Presence or Pure Consciousness. That's the point where the Ultimate Subjectivity begins to *feel* itself. Here is the bridge between the Source and the manifestation. The Ultimate is prior to it.

Before the unmanifested is realized, the essence of consciousness must be realized. What is that which is reaching this realization? It is the operative self-conscious center of consciousness, which in our case is recognized as the personality or the ego. Ego is the self-conscious movement of our intelligence without which there is no spiritual search and no Enlightenment. Personality is the manifested aspect of reality. Initially it is directed towards the exploration of the external world. But when it is directed inwardly, personality can create a conscious bridge between the external reality and the source of manifestation. This is what is called Awakening.

The Presence and the Absolute

Presence is nothing but the awakened essence of manifestation. When the manifestation is unconscious it is completely confined to how it *appears* to be; it is purely identified with its own objectivization. Presence is being manifested but it is not in the manifestation. It is neither emptiness nor form, but something in-between. Consciousness can have three orientations: it can be present to the manifested, which is life; it can be present to itself, which is Presence; and it can be present simultaneously to the manifested and to itself, which is Witnessing. Apart from this, we have the state of no-orientation, which is *being* in the Absolute.

From the perspective of thoughts, the operating intelligence is in the center of consciousness (illusion of ego); from the perspective of operating intelligence, the Presence is the center. This Presence knows itself as a feeling of being, as a non-dual awareness. When the consciousness shifts from personality to its own nature, it stops in itself. In this stop it knows itself as itself.

The dimension of Beingness, from which the consciousness arises is called the Absolute. The Absolute never appears. It can not appear, for to whom could it present itself? The *seer* precedes the seen. Of course the Ultimate seer is not an entity but a potential of all that can be seen. When we speak about non-dual perception, we must remember that unless that which makes everything possible is realized, the true meaning of this concept has not been understood yet. The Absolute can not be an object of perception, can not *appear* to be, because it is the foundation which allows the appearance of everything else. While the manifestation *appears* to be, the Absolute is already to appear as consciousness. What this means is that the Absolute can only be manifested as consciousness, and in itself forever remains the *Unmanifested.* It is the timeless, sacred vessel of time, space and consciousness— but in itself is Beyond.

Realization of the Absolute belongs to consciousness; it is the function of the manifested. The realization of the Absolute is the fifth dimension. Before this is possible, the forth dimension must be reached, which is the Essence of Consciousness. Although we might regard Presence as not being in time, for it is unceasingly present to the Now, when we go deeper into its nature we see that the touch of time is there. It might seem that Presence knows itself instantaneously, but actually this recognition happens in a split of second—it is a function of a subtle time. One needs to be sensitive enough to see it. Presence is the point at which the Unmanifested touches the manifested, which is time. When consciousness wakes up to itself, the state of Presence is realized; when the state of Presence wakes up, the Unborn is realized.

How does the Presence, which is touched by time, reach the timeless? It is a mystery. There is a realization which encompasses the knowing of consciousness and the not-knowing of the Unmanifested: the experience of being present and the absence of presence. This realization is truly beyond all that we know. The Absolute can be compared to the sun, while Witnessing to its rays. The realization takes place at their meeting point; before the sun becomes its rays there is a secret gap where the knowing of the Absolute is born. The only way to reach the Absolute is surrender. One must drop the center of Presence into the non-center of non-presence. We call it *de-centralization*. Moving through different layers of consciousness, we see more and more clearly that it cannot rest. It cannot rest even at the point of Presence, for it has a constant creative impulse–a will to move, to become... No wonder it is the essence of time. Only that which is not *of time* can be at complete rest. The Absolute is the Rest itself.

When practicing absorption, we make an attempt to renounce the will. Falling with our breath into the total letting go of any will, we see that at the bottom of the breath, where the exhalation is completed there is a *stop*. The Presence, falling with the breath, drops into itself; but although it drops into itself, it cannot sustain this split second of not-doing; it gets *suffocated* with itself and has to move, has to fluctuate. It cannot rest in non-doing. Only when we fully understand consciousness, are we ready to receive Grace, which responds to our surrender. Only thanks to Grace, can we enter into the Absolute State—into this bottomless Rest. It is truly amazing! That which seems to be impossible becomes true. Suddenly we are in a place which is not touched by any of the functions of consciousness. We rest absolutely.

This is the true meaning of non-abiding. There is no change in this state, which is *no-state*. This mysterious *knowing*, which allows us to know that the Unborn has been realized—is *beyond*. This tremendous freedom which takes place in consciousness is freedom *from* consciousness. It is the completion of our Path toward the Ultimate Subjectivity. The Unborn, Unbecome, Uncreated, Unmanifested has received us, full of our infinite longing, into its Eternal home of Peace.

Meditation

Meditation is the art of transcending the mind with the mind. What we mean is that human consciousness, using its inherent intelligence can reach a much deeper experience of Being then the mental realm. Ultimately, meditation is a state of being and not a state of doing, but to transcend the mind's ignorance, certain elements must be introduced.

Consciousness is a form of attention. Normally this attention is dispersed in mental activity, which turns the beautiful human intelligence into an unconscious, mechanical and ignorant mass of chaos. To develop the quality of alertness, we might utilize various objects of focus. For example, observation of the breath, body sensations or arising of thoughts. We call it alertness to the object. The alertness is somehow connected with the center of consciousness in the mind. That's why when it is strengthened and prolonged, it directly affects the middle of the head, and slowly begins the process of awakening one from the day-dream state. We need to remember that it is an indirect path; in the case of a mature person, the center of consciousness can be awakened directly.

There are two aspects of mindfulness: mindfulness of an object and mindfulness of the center. Mindfulness of the center is, of course, our goal. Whatever observation is chosen for the meditation, it is just a tool. We can say that any meditation on an object, whether it is breath, mind, body or feelings, is a semi-meditation or negative meditation. "Negative" because it refers to the object and not to the subject. The object always belongs to the past. It is only the subject, the attention prior to perception, that belongs to Now.

When the consciousness is not ready to recognize its center, we must first prepare the ground. Observation of the breath, of the mind and so forth develop certain areas within the conscious mind, so finally it can click into the state of self-attention. Developing the awareness of what is occurring in our mind and body transforms one at last into a conscious being. From the human robot, the human being is awakened. This is a stage where one is becoming conscious, but still not self-conscious in the right sense of this term.

What is that which is mindful of an object? When this question is asked within ourselves, the mindfulness for the first time refers to itself, attention becomes attentive to itself and one finds oneself in the center of consciousness. This is what the proper Satori, the scientific Satori should look like. Clarity, wisdom and simplicity are the qualities of this state. The proper meditation starts at this point. The inquiry supports meditation but meditation goes beyond it, always beyond it.

When the "I Am" blossoms in the middle of our being, we can be fairly content. At least we have some ground under our feet. No longer are we groping in the darkness searching for miraculous Enlightenment. "I Am" is what I Am. The experience of myself becomes solidified. Now one is learning how to retain the sense of I Am in meditation and in all situations, so slowly it becomes the real center of one's life. In meditation one is learning how to keep the center of Presence, how to be constantly mindful of it. This mindfulness is opening this center more and more, so it starts to be aware of itself automatically. That's why we also call it "witnessing," for it just "happens to be there" although nobody has invited it. It is like blowing on the fire until suddenly it catches by itself and is "witnessing" whatever we do. It is that simple.

Mindfulness or alertness is an energy that is strongly affecting the center of consciousness. When this center is awakened, the mindfulness directed towards it, affects it even more strongly. The presence of the center transforms gradually the function of the mind. In due time it becomes more and more emptied of content. But this is not our purpose; it is what is occurring naturally. The inner economy of silence and thinking creates the right balance. In this balance the thoughts still come as a natural function of the mind, but their momentum is very slow as if they were flowing within the silence. However, it takes time for the mind to adjust, and in the beginning of this process the subconscious may even produce more thoughts.

On one hand, we learn how to retain the state of Presence and on the other, how to be with the state, how to sit in it. Now we are entering the realm of Shikan-taza or pure meditation. When one is aware of the Presence, it is like the feeling of waking up in this very moment. There is a sort of gentle movement within our inner state as if the observing intelligence was meeting its inner Presence. It is as if they were one and two at the same time. In the state of meditation, the observing consciousness becomes relaxed and the state of Presence can rest upon itself. This is what we call just sitting or Shikan-taza. The practitioner checks very gently from time to time, whether the inner center is present, and simultaneously drops into the non-doing, into the state emptied of the personal will.

In reality, it is not so much about the elimination of personal will, but about adding that which simply is at the background. The state of Presence has a will of its own. It is the will of energy within the silence, within the emptiness. When the personal will surrenders to the state of Presence, the economy of attention becomes immediately transformed. The mind is still functioning in a subtle way, but the awareness of resting in the center of Presence contains the personal will within the space of something much bigger. The mind is almost shy to think in the presence of the all-witnessing "I Am" consciousness. But we should not think that there is no will in the state of Shikan-taza. There is will, but it is transformed; the will of personality is resting upon the will of silence.

Let's see what the possible mental activities in the Shikan-taza are. There can be a passive arising of thoughts that come and go; the meditator is unmoved resting in the stillness of the I Am. When the intelligence of the meditator chooses, consciously or spontaneously, to participate in the action of thoughts, the will is active again. This is fully acceptable as long as the I Am state is present. In meditation, we consciously choose to minimize the personal will, surrendering to the inner stillness, but we cannot eliminate it completely if we desire to remain conscious. The will is a part of consciousness, and as we will see, even the state of Presence carries the element of subtle will.

When the Presence is awakened, there is an immediate transformation in the functioning of our consciousness. Whether we think consciously or not, the mental activity does not touch the stillness of the center. How we are operating with our mental energy does not change the presence of the center but does change the quality of it. The state of Presence, although witnessing the mental dimension in a naturally detached way, at the same time is being directly affected by the direction of personal attention. That's why we have different levels of absorption, for example. It is not just the Presence absorbed in the Presence. It is the conscious energy of personality surrendering to the inner state that gives rise to the deeper and deeper experience of samadhi.

We can say that there are actually two centers present in the inner reality of the meditator. One is the state of Presence, which in the case of an integrated person is constant. Second is the center of personal will. These two centers are affecting each other constantly. The personal will is always witnessed by the state of Presence. On the other hand, how the personal attention relates to the Presence immediately changes the quality of this state. So in Shikan-taza, the will of personal intelligence is not eliminated, but minimized to the level of experiencing deep rest and non-doing as a foundation. We can call it a minimum ego.

For the non-doing to occur, the energy of personality must have a place of abiding. In consciousness, the non-abiding cannot take place. The only place where the personality can be freed from itself is the silent background of Presence. The personality can rest only in the I Am. The I Am is not separated from personality, but is beyond it.

Keeping the sense of I Am until it becomes spontaneously constant, and learning how to rest in it are the two foundations of meditation, of Shikan-taza. Using gentle observation, we learn how our mind and the state of Presence co-exist and relate to each other. We learn about the economy of attention and the economy of will. We learn how the personal will and the stillness of I Am can be simultaneously present. We get more and more in touch with the complexity and beauty of the inner world of the Self.

This world is not at all static. It is a dynamic dance of silence, energy and intelligence. Practicing meditation, one needs to be extremely focused and sensitive. Meditation is an art form that takes us beyond ignorance. It is the essence of life. Whoever enters this path, truly for the first time enters life.

Beyond Vipassana

Does Vipassana liberate? The Insight Meditation is one of the meditation techniques left by the Buddha in his compassion for those who desire freedom. However, no technique can be the <u>absolute</u> means for arriving at the Enlightened state, because techniques only deal with ignorance and never with the Truth itself. Removing ignorance and the awakening to the truth, though interconnected, are not the same. On the path to Enlightenment one often has to utilize some skillful means, but the Awakening is not a simple outcome of our efforts. The reality of the Inner State is unknown until the moment when one clearly experiences it. Our challenge is to bridge ignorance and Enlightenment. It is not a simple task, for we intend to reach the transcendental state from the perspective of our limited consciousness. How can it be done? The awakening is a function of the Now, and all our indirect methods are only a preparation for the moment when we are ready to face the truth of our ultimate identity.

The foundation of Insight meditation is the conviction that by seeing clearly the world and our psycho-somatic identity as having no self, no permanence and being basically painful, we reach somehow automatically the right understanding and liberation. How often we experience these insights in our daily life and nothing happens? Developing active observation and trying to reach certain conceptual disidentification during meditation is a very dangerous technique, for one remains at all time on the level of the mind.

Is meditation only negative? Is the purpose of meditation only to realize that all is an illusion? When we see the statue of Buddha isn't it obvious that he reached something extremely positive? Buddha not only said that there is nothing permanent in this world, he also said that there is the Unborn. He said clearly that if there was no Unborn there wouldn't be any possibility of liberation. *The Enlightenment and the interpretation of reality based on Enlightenment are not the same.* The Vipassana practitioner tries to reach certain Buddhist philosophical conclusions without being in the Enlightened state, hoping that when those conclusion-insights are fully realized, he/she becomes automatically liberated. This however, is an illusion.

We must see clearly that the Vipassana insights are occurring only in the mind. It is the mind which is observing the mind and the mind certainly cannot go beyond itself, for it always operates in the psychological past. Understanding is important, but it cannot liberate; it doesn't have the power of transcendence.

The teaching about the no-self needs be used intelligently. This teaching is not a dogma but a tool dealing with certain tendencies of the human mind. The concept that there is actually "nobody" who meditates, "nobody" who has an insight and "nobody" who becomes Enlightened is correct only from a certain point of view and incorrect from another. The reality of Enlightenment is beyond the concept of "self" and "no-self" as well. Behind the movement of intelligence, thoughts and feelings there is a transcendental state of Being which has to be awakened. Disidentification doesn't liberate, understanding doesn't liberate—it is the expansion into the Real which liberates. When

Buddha experienced his great Enlightenment under the Boddhi tree he not only had an insight into the nature of illusion-he actually shifted into the new dimension of being which is the Unborn Source of manifestation. It is neither the self nor the no-self—it doesn't have a name but it is absolutely real!

Let us repeat the first conclusion: if Vipassana ends as an insight into impermanence, no-self and suffering-it certainly doesn't liberate. For the same reason, most psycho-therapies nowadays do not work. One becomes only aware of one's negativity and neurotic tendencies and this awareness in itself doesn't have the power of transformation. It is always the positive which transforms. We don't strive to become disidentified for the sake of disidentification. The disidentification points to something beyond. The "beyond" is not simply an absence of the negativity and illusion. The "beyond" is a dimension of its own, and it represents the quality of absolute positivity. The Awakened One is not only free from suffering-he/she is in the state of inner fulfillment and bliss.

This fulfillment is not merely satisfaction from leaving this world behind, it is a transcendental state. A state exalted within itself. It is very difficult in the context of the "no-self" theory to describe the positive quality of the essence of the Buddha Mind. It is very interesting how a concept can, in a dogmatic way, control our means of expression. Whatever one says, one will be accused of the false belief in the self. *Liberation exists not because the false is seen as false but because and only because the Truth is seen as the Truth.* It is the positive that liberates. And it truly doesn't matter whether we call it being or non-being, or both or neither—the positive, the Truth, the Buddha Nature simply *is*.

The question arises, how can we make a quantum

leap from "negative" insight meditation to positive
Enlightenment? How can we go beyond Vipassana? It
is not that Vipassana is not a useful meditation
technique, for it is. It is a tool to be used, but we must
see the limits of this tool. It has its beauty and usefulness,
but at some stage needs to be dropped, as any other
technique does. The Unknown can only be entered
naked. So how to move forward?

The secret lies in the very attention which is observing
the mind. All that is arising in the mind is ceasing as
well. When the attention, which is the seed of every
conscious action of the mind, suddenly turns upon
itself, one finds oneself at the zero point of experience.
That zero point is called the state of Presence. Negative
meditation is concerned only with the object, with the
observed, while positive meditation points always to this
mysterious "place" from which the observation arises.
The subject, which is the essence of meditation, is not
the ego but the primordial direct experience of isness.

The state of Presence directly recognizes itself without
the medium of mind. We can call it the center of
consciousness, preceding always its phenomenal
expressions. For anyone who is completely integrated
with the state of Presence, it is experienced in every
moment as an unceasing flow of self-recognizing
awareness. Some masters take it for the ultimate state.
It is not so. It is rather a link between the mind and
the Unborn. In India they call it "Atman." This state is
extremely important, because in it the unconscious
mind becomes transcended. This state is already beyond
any kind of understanding or insights created within
the mind.

From the observation and mindfulness of the
phenomenal reality we shift into the dimension of
being. We can say that at that moment Vipassana turns

into Shikan-taza. Shikan-taza is not a Zen technique but a universal state of consciousness. The meaning of Shikan-taza is: "just being," that is, "non-doing while being conscious." The "non-doing" is possible only if there is a place where our consciousness can dwell and rest; only if there is a place in which the automatic will of our conscious mind can be suspended and released. "Just sitting" cannot take place unless the movement of psyche expands beyond its frame of reference into the deeper level of existing. That which allows us at this stage to go beyond our psyche is the state of Presence.

From the point of view of one who is in the state of Presence, it feels like an experience of absolute subjectivity. To prove that this is so, some practitioners try even to bring this state to the Sleep State. But this is unwise, for to be aware during sleep ultimately can create serious imbalance in the psyche. The presence of awareness during Sleep State interferes with the natural healing process of our subconscious. To know when to control and when to let go is a function of intelligence. There is no need to control the sleep state, as there is no need to control the moment of death, when all dissolves into the Source and there is no force in the universe that can stop it.

The state of Presence, called also rigpa in Dzogchen or clear mind in Zen, is not the ultimate, and finally has to be transcended. Nevertheless we have to see that this state already has the quality of the positive. It has the quality of semi-constant experience, of bliss and peace. It is only semi-constant because, although it is beyond the mind, yet still it belongs to the realm of energy which has the characteristic of movement and fluctuation. It is only deep sensitivity and intelligence that allows us to see the relative character of this state. Seeing this we can go deeper.

Although we spoke about the state of non-doing (for the personal will rests within the state of Presence), in reality the subtle will is still operating on this level. The energy of consciousness, of the Presence, has a will of its own, that on the subtle level is interwoven with the will of our psyche. We can say that resting in the State of Presence gives us merely an experience of relative, incomplete Shikan-taza. The absolute Shikan-taza, pure being or non-doing, can take place only when the state of Presence is transcended. We can only speak about reaching the absolute subjectivity at that moment: the non-abiding ground of all existence. The state of Presence is still abiding, in its own center.

The final shift has a very mysterious nature. When the center of attention which is the state of Presence, expands into the original timeless sphere of pre-attention, into the non-aware womb of manifestation, the realm of empty origin-the final expansion takes place. Afterward, there is no longer any center, for one is resting in the state prior to experience, prior to awareness. Certainly there is a recognition of the Unborn which creates a new quality that comes from the meeting of the Presence with the Absolute (the non-presence state). This recognition is extremely subtle and can be described as a knowingness of pure rest without any center. It is here that our Presence as a center of consciousness, that is, pure attention, meets the Unborn, the primordial source of all.

This meeting gives birth to the experience of pure, motionless rest. The totality of our consciousness becomes one with the absolute timeless Void. And not only does one realize "what has been there always," but the very fact of our recognition gives rise to something that is totally new. It is the flowering of evolution. The light of awareness enters the pre-aware source of creation. And truly this is what all beings are longing for. It is not to drop the manifested reality, but to enter and rest in our original home of bottomless peace. From that place, even impermanence is seen as beautiful. All is finally embraced.

Mindfulness: Of What?

Paying attention to the environment is one of the basic meditation tools for awakening. Mindfulness means that one is <u>conscious</u> of certain area of one's experience. The object of mindfulness doesn't need to be the external reality. One can be mindful of one's own mind as well. The activity of being "conscious of" is very interesting. What does it mean to be "conscious of?" It means that there is already a touch of the Presence behind the process of experiencing. This touch of Presence is still not self-conscious, but there is a knowing that one is present to the experience.

We can speak about mindfulness or "consciousness of" as a passage from the unconscious, objectified psyche to the state of Presence. Mindfulness somehow roots us in reality, freeing the psyche from mechanical mental activity. To be free from the mind, which is excessively active in all human beings, we have got to either become completely numb and unconscious or start paying attention, that is becoming "conscious of."

We can use various objects of mindfulness. We can be mindful of the external reality and our activity. We can pay attention to our body, its movements or sensations. We can be conscious of the breath. And we can become mindful of our own mind.

As far as transformation is concerned, the awareness of the breath is very important. Particularly, mindfulness combined with slow and deep breathing to the belly can have a very strong impact on the mind and the transmutation of energy. Unless the energy of our being is balanced and transformed, to reach any of the inner states is practically impossible.

But if we are going to choose the object of mindfulness from the viewpoint of the awakening itself, we would choose the mind. Why the mind? For the very simple reason that the attention is generated in the mind and the thinking process is the nearest to the center of watchfulness. For most people, to become aware of thinking is already a big step. To be able to create a distance and space between the "watcher" and the thinking process is extremely important. Most everyone is able, more or less, to become aware of one's surroundings, body sensations or the breath, but to be conscious of one's mind, is for most people, a very difficult task. It is simply too close to Me.

Becoming conscious of the content of the mind is used here for the process of awakening, not for psychological work. At this point, it is not what we think that matters, but the distance between Me and the thought. Because the center of attention is not fully awakened yet, one still experiences difficulties in grasping that which is conscious of the mind. When we are able to turn the attention back to itself, it becomes self—conscious.

Mindfulness oscillates between the areas we are becoming "conscious of" and being "self-conscious." Becoming "conscious of" is the Here and being self-conscious is the Now. They are not the same. The awakening refers to the state where the attention recognizes itself, that is, becomes self-conscious. It is here that the state of Presence is born.

Here and Now

Is being "here and now" all that is required in order to experience the awakened state? This simple description of the meditative mind, although correct, can be quite misleading. From the view point of one who has reached the Absolute State, "chopping wood and caring water" is a possible way of expressing the Enlightened state of mind. But certainly it is not the case for someone who has not completed the inner work.

To be "in the moment" is not the same as being in the Truth. The Truth is a unity of the subjective and objective polarities of existence. One can be perfectly in the moment without any connection with the state of Presence. In this case, one is Here but not Now.

The Here refers to empirical time, to the experience of being aware of external reality. The Here is a mixture of the perceived and the element of being "aware of." It is the element of being "aware of" that makes us feel "Here." In this case, one experiences a level of freedom from the mind and a connection with empirical reality.

What is the Now? While Here refers to the awareness of our connection to the objective reality, Now in truth points to the subjective reality, to the I Am. Now is not the act of drinking tea, for example, but one's own Presence within this act. When the Now is grasped fully, the Here can be forgotten. The Now is a foundation and the essence of our practice.

To connect more deeply to the state of Presence, we often need to withdraw our attention from the environment. We pull the attention inward, intensifying it only to the extent in which we can retain our center within the outer reality. When the state of Presence is grasped firmly, we can let go of inner concentration and relax into the Here. In this way, the inner (the state of Presence) and the outer are experienced more and more as one. But until one is stabilized in the Presence, the need to pull back from the outer naturally arises, from time to time; when the energetic presence of the I Am loses its strength. The energy of attention intensifies the state of Presence and one experiences the clarity and strength of the inner center. It is important to know that unless one is stabilized in the I Am, it is not possible to be fully Here and Now. Prior to stabilization, one oscillates between the Now and the Here. To experience fully and effortlessly the Here and Now as a unity, we need let go of the inner focus, which is possible only after stabilization.

Awareness of the objective and subjective realities is not the same. For this reason, the teaching of "being in the moment" is not fully sufficient for those who are at the beginning of the path. For these, the awakening to the state of Presence is much more important than "chopping wood and carrying water." This awakening points primarily to the area of subjectivity, that is, to how "I" experience myself directly, prior to the perception of the outer. Before we can relax fully into the Here, the center of subjectivity must be reached.

Are Koans the Universal Language of Enlightenment?

We may be surprised to know that being in the Enlightened State does not automatically enable one to respond "properly" to Zen questions or intellectual challenges. These challenges are also present in other traditions. One is expected to answer in a certain way, to specific questions according to the philosophy and convention of the particular school of Enlightenment, in order to qualify one's attainment. But we may ask an important question: is there a universal language of Enlightenment?

The relationship between the Enlightened State and the psyche that experiences it, is very complex. How the Awakened being responds to the environment and what kind of understanding he/she expresses depends on many factors. It is not the inner state alone that creates our perception of reality. The inner state adds to the psyche the background of silence and stillness, but the perception itself is formed within the mind and channeled through our sensitivity. We cannot simply define a fixed standard of speech and behavior for all who are in the Enlightened State. The intelligence and sensitivity of <u>each Soul</u> is unique and must be respected.

The danger of certain traditions is that they attempt to condition everyone according to their models of reality. Particularly in the schools of Zen that use the Koan system, the process of shaping a certain type of personality goes to the extreme. The Zen training of Koans can be highly damaging for the Soul, which is sensitive and delicate. This training is based on the preconception that unless one responds to the Zen challenges in a very sharp and masculine way, according to the set convention, one is not in a "right" state of mind. However useful the Koan system is to concentrate the mind and transmit a certain highly sophisticated vision of reality, it is merely an angle of the expression of Truth. No "angle" of perception of truth can possibly be established as the absolute referential point to verify the attainment of Truth.

It is possible that someone with a sharp mind may be able to answer perfectly a Koan without being in the state of Presence. On the other hand, it is possible that someone may not be capable of responding to any Koans, though rooted in the Absolute State. Why is this? For the very simple reason that the Koans are not the universal language of Enlightenment. And as mentioned, there can never be a universal language of Enlightenment, only a unique individual expression of the Universal Truth.

The Koan system may be helpful for those who have a certain type of mind and personality. In the case of the one who is not ready to see directly the essence of Consciousness, a Koan can be used as a means of concentration and inspiration for inquiry. In this case, one attempts to manifest the correct response as if one were in the awakened state. It is similar to the Vipassana practitioner who tries to perceive the Buddha conclusions without being in the Buddha State.

The Koan system is not universal. It has its beauty as a Zen art form and certainly can be beneficial. But by its very nature it can highly limit our individual expression. Therefore, a matured practitioner, at a certain point needs to transcend this conditioning of perception in order to evolve further into the New. The ultimate perception is born when the complete realization of the Inner Reality, that is, Enlightenment meets fully the unique sensitivity and intelligence of an individual Soul. This is called maturity.

The language of Enlightenment is not a formula but subject to evolution. This evolution is related to the creativity of many Souls who are seeking their unique perception and expression within the context of Enlightenment. We should not forget that the highest proof of one's attainment is not in one's behavior or cleverness in speech and action. The Inner Truth expresses itself through our being, heart and energy. In reality Enlightenment cannot be proved. But it is how others feel around the Self-realized being, and how their consciousness is affected that make them believe that he/she is in the transcendental state. In the case of the master-disciple relationship, when there is love and right connection, the master is able to recognize directly the inner state of the disciple. No special checking system is needed. This is the essence of the profound spirit of Transmission.

Reaching the Absolute Rest

After stabilization in the state of Presence, one needs to receive teaching in order to shift to the Ultimate. This teaching cannot be found in books, for it hasn't been elaborated yet by any master or tradition. It is very difficult to speak about it, for the experience is unique and subtle, beyond imagination. It can be transmitted only in the atmosphere of deep love, sincerity and openness between the disciple and the master. It doesn't need to be a human master. The highest state is rare. On this planet only very few people are blessed to be in it. Even among the masters it is rare to reach the Ultimate. Why is that? Because it is the Ultimate!

As we already spoke about, even the state of Presence is operating within the subtle will. It is the will of consciousness to recreate itself in every moment; it is the will of energy to create, to move, to fluctuate. This will is interconnected with the personal will, because the I Am and the ego, although not the same, are not separated. For that reason, resting in the state of Presence is still not an absolute Shikan-taza. It is still occurring in the dimension of the manifested. It is deeper than the personal mind but is not deeper than the manifestation.

Now we will attempt to discover the complete meaning of Shikan-taza, the absolute Shikan-taza. It cannot take place unless consciousness is transcended. That which takes us beyond the will and movement is only the Absolute, the original state. How to find the link between the state of Presence and the timeless Source? This link is called expansion. It takes us beyond the I Am without annihilating the experience of being conscious. When one loses consciousness, one is in the Absolute, but without knowing it, so it doesn't have any use for the individual. That which makes the Absolute an Exalted state is the presence of consciousness, which is like the light entering the void of nothingness. The Absolute is an absence of consciousness and consciousness is the absence of knowing the Absolute. When the realization of the Absolute State takes place, these two apparently opposite dimensions melt with each other. Within the consciousness, the knowing of the Absolute is born, the knowing of the unknowable. The miracle takes place. But let's look at this matter with a more practical eye.

When one realizes clearly that meditation is occurring in the realm of consciousness, which represents in itself the quality of will, the question arises as to how one can transcend this limitation. The center of consciousness, the I Am, cannot release itself from its inherent fluctuations. Because of this center, one can transcend the mind, but even within the I Am it is not possible to be completely at ease. One still must go deeper. How can we reach the no-will state? How can we find the ultimate freedom which is the absence of oneself, without losing consciousness?

The mind cannot grasp it. Only the clear experience allows us to know it fully. This experience can take place only through Grace; Grace in the form of transmission. This transmission can come from a master who is in the Absolute State or from the other dimension, from the Beyond. To reach the I Am one can use the will, even though the final stabilization happens also through Grace. To reach the Ultimate, the will is not enough, for the will cannot transcend itself. It is only Grace that can open the secret gate. This is the meaning of "transmission from mind to mind." The love and intention of the master meet the devotion, love and surrender of the disciple, and the transmission of the state takes place. But the transmission of the Ultimate state can take place only if the disciple is ready and the timing is right. Grace, in a sense, is scientific and not blind. The transmission can be received if there is maturity of consciousness, maturity of energy and sincerity of heart. The fruit must be ripe in order to drop to the Absolute.

The shift to the Absolute does not always include the stabilization in it. The shift is called the Awakening and the stabilization is called Enlightenment. Usually after the awakening, time is needed for the energy to adjust. The shift to the Absolute can be a traumatic experience for the body because the frequency of energy increases to the maximum and the body cannot deal with it. So time is necessary to gradually transform the structure of the physical and energy bodies. When the stabilization takes place, the energy of the Absolute State which enters through the Crown chakra, drops completely to the Hara. This is the point from which the Absolute State cannot be lost, for the energy of all being is constantly focused within it.

Although the realization of the Ultimate takes place through Transmission, the cooperation from the part of the practitioner is extremely important. What is this cooperation about? The Transmission is coming from without and the readiness to receive it is coming from within. The opening of the gate to the state of Pure Rest and the act of slipping into it, are not separated from each other. A most subtle surrender within the state of Presence takes us beyond the dimension of consciousness, that is, beyond the dimension of will. This surrender is itself an expansion, for without expansion there is no surrender.

When sitting in absorption and contemplating the state of Presence, the clarity arises: this is not the Ultimate! Compared with the mind, the state of Presence is seen as peace and stillness, but compared with the Absolute, the Presence is perceived as an incomplete state representing the qualities of restlessness and necessity to fluctuate. It is not merely that the state of Presence has got to move. It is Me, who is one with the state of Presence that must move. The state of Presence can be described as a constant act of will. It is being born in every moment as an act of will, followed immediately by the next act of will. It is a very subtle will, the will of consciousness. It simply cannot rest. Because at this stage the Presence has become my identity-it is Me who cannot rest, it is Me who is a part of this automatic will of consciousness that must recreate itself from moment to moment.

Consciousness lives only through movement. Without movement there is no consciousness. It applies fully to "thoughtless awareness" as well. There is no escape from it. Every act of the state of Presence is an act of will. This will is Me—this has to be clear. That's why the concept of "witnessing consciousness" is, in a way, incorrect. The state of Presence, although witnessing the personality, is at the same time Me, for my center of identity dwells in these two dimensions. Because I am the Presence, I am caught in its movement. In every act of Presence, it recreates itself, it gives birth to itself. The state of Presence is a movement within time.

What is this which wishes to rest in the state of Presence? What is this which is identified with the Presence and is experiencing frustration, for this state cannot free itself from its movement? We know that the traditional answer is "nobody." However, this answer does not apply in reality. In truth I am not the state of Presence. I am that which wants to rest in it. That which experiences all states is neither Consciousness nor the Absolute. It is Me, the Soul.

Sitting in absorption, we rest at the bottom of the Presence. This is a very interesting point. One drops into the state of Presence, surrendering completely the will, but at the same time one is overtaken by the next momentum of consciousness that recreates itself. The act of dropping into the non-doing affects directly the Presence, as if it reaches the minimum of its will, as if it dropped into the non-doing as well. But all of this can occur only for a short moment, for the Presence gets "suffocated" with the suspension of will and must create within itself a new movement, a new act of consciousness; one cannot rest in the state of Presence. All one can do is to repeat the act of surrendering the volition and drop into the bottom of the experience of Presence. In this act, the surrender encounters the inherent will of the Presence to recreate its conscious recognition. It is like hitting the wall. It seems that there is no way of breaking through the walls of consciousness. But this surrendering is very important, for it allows us to become more and more sensitive to that which the consciousness is, what the Presence is and what the will is. The will is a fundamental quality of consciousness. So the Soul cannot find true rest within the dimension of Presence.

At one stage, the surrender of the Soul encounters an opening within the state of Presence. In this opening the Soul slips into the Absolute. The "amness" of the Presence is a doorway to the "isness" of the Absolute. The Soul uses the clear, alert amness to expand and reach the Absolute. The Presence belongs to the Soul, the amness belongs to the Soul, but the Soul herself is something else. It is the Soul that feels the Presence as a part of herself and rests upon the Absolute. The Presence is the amness of the Soul, but the Soul herself represents other qualities as well. It is the mysterious Me, the I, the mysterious subject, the seer behind all states.

The desire to go beyond the will is the will of the Soul. The Soul herself is not free from the will so she cannot rest within herself. She needs to expand to that which is her foundation, her ultimate abiding, to find freedom from will. She cannot find this freedom within the Presence, for the amness also has the essential quality of will. The will of the Presence is, in a way, being experienced by the Soul as its own will, for she is on some level, identified with her amness. It is truly amazing to see how the Presence and the Me who reaches it are two and one at the same time. When the Soul is not awakened to herself she tends to be completely identified with the amness. She interprets the amness as her center and true identity. When the clarity arises that the Presence is not sufficient to reach freedom from manifestation and will, when the seeing arises that in the realm of amness there is no true peace and rest, the Soul creates the desire to go deeper.

How does the Soul know that there exists a state deeper than the Presence? There are many elements. One is trust in the revelation from another Soul, such as a master, or from the Guidance from Beyond. Another element relates to the fact that because the Absolute State is both the timeless foundation of the Soul and her future conscious realization, there is an intuitive link, a subtle knowing which bridges the seeker and the sought.

So the desire to reach the will-less state, the Pure Rest, is the will of the Soul. It seems contradictory in terms that one can reach the will-less using will. However, there is no conflict if we truly understand what is happening. Because the traditional teachings negated the existence of the "one" who reaches the Ultimate, they couldn't get out of this paradox. The desire to reach the state of Pure Rest is like knocking at the gate of the Ultimate. The point where the Presence reaches its furthest limits, its deepest bottom, is the place where one reality ends and the second might enter. We speak about the moment in absorption when one surrenders the will and drops into pure Non-doing state, into Shikan-taza. When the will is dropped through the channel of Presence, the beingness of the Presence reaches its limits. So far, the will can be surrendered only to the state of Presence for it is the deepest root of our beingness. As we already spoke of, within the Presence, the No-will state, the Shikan-taza can be experienced only for a split second. The state of Presence gets immediately suffocated in the no-will condition, so it creates a new wave of movement—it becomes the will again.

The moment of suspension of movement in the absorption can be seen as a tiny moment of rest between two sequential acts of will. The Soul's act of surrender, the very fact of dropping into the absorption with the intention of being in a state of Non-doing, gives a longer momentum to this suspension, as if putting a weight on the state of Presence. This weight is the surrender of the Soul; the Soul has her own weight of being that can be directed towards different areas of consciousness.

The decision of the Soul to transcend the will is not enough, however it is important in preparing the ground for future expansion. Still, by itself it cannot break through the thick wall of consciousness. The decision of the Soul to transcend the consciousness and her effort to break the momentum of the self-generating will, must encounter, at one stage, the Grace from the Beyond. This is the Grace from the Absolute itself. Something needs to enter. Something must open so that Pure Rest can be manifested.

In Pure Rest the Soul can fully, effortlessly and unconditionally rest upon the primordial original void, free from change and fluctuations of consciousness. Grace is not accidental; there is a law behind it. The maturity of the Soul, the sincerity of the heart, destiny and right timing are the essential elements which must be present. The destiny of the Soul is in the good hands of the all encompassing wisdom and love of Universal Intelligence and the power of evolution. This is nothing but the Beloved herself.

At the moment of shifting to the Absolute State, the Soul does not change her identity. She expands into the dimension of Pure Rest. Something is added to her, the Foundation, the place of Ultimate Abidance. The Soul still has an element of will, but the dimension of no-will has been added. This allows us to grasp the apparent paradox of using the will and being beyond it at the same time. The no-will state is a foundation; the will is an expression. It is like the movement of the tree and the motionlessness of its roots—they are one.

Three Pillars of Reaching
the Absolute State

The three pillars of reaching the Absolute State are:

Awakening (the shift);
Stabilization; and
Integration.

In the Awakening, the passage to the Absolute has become open, and one is capable of slipping into it from time to time. But although the passage is open in the Crown chakra, the energy is not fully pulled to the Hara. Although many traditions speak about pulling the Kundalini energy upward, in reality the final completion involves the turning of that energy downward into the Hara. The gravitational force of the Absolute pulls everything in. So only after the radical shift of the energy into the Hara, can we speak about the constant presence of the Absolute. The Stabilization directs this energy constantly into the Absolute. After the Stabilization, some time is needed for the Integration to take place. In Integration, the recognition of the Absolute and the energy are in complete alignment.

The Recognition of the Absolute

The Absolute State transcends the totality of consciousness, taking us beyond the most direct touch of beingness, the I Am, the primordial experience of Presence. The Absolute State is the dimension of meeting of the I Am with the Absolute. The shift to the Absolute brings about the most subtle state of transparent knowingness in which the being and the non-being become unified. When the Source receives within itself the essence of knowing, that is, our innate pure Presence, the meeting of the Creation and the Unborn takes place.

What gives splendor to this meeting is not only its very occurrence, but the power of recognition. It is this power of recognition which gives life to the realization of the Absolute State. It is not true that all who shift to the Absolute experience it in the same way. There are even those who do not know that the state has been realized or that it is even a "state." There are those who, after this realization, still see no difference between the Absolute and the Presence. All of this is governed by the power of recognition-that which embraces the experience of Enlightenment. There is the shift into the Absolute and there is the recognition of it–they are not the same. There cannot be, of course, any recognition without the shift but there can be shift without recognition. Recognition is like a light that makes things visible; without the light even the most precious diamond cannot be seen. Realization of the

Absolute is like entering a dark room; recognition is
like turning the light on. What is that which allows us
to recognize the Absolute State? It is nothing but the
sensitivity of the Soul and its intuitive intelligence. The
recognition is the pure wisdom of direct knowing. It
sees, discerns and understands.

What actually happens at the moment of shift to the
Absolute? The energy of the Presence expands into the
original state of non-presence. This expansion happens
to the Presence as if it had melted into its own original
absence without losing the quality of attention. So
when the Presence expands, the center of one's identity
drops to the state of absence, pushing the very
experience of any modification of consciousness to the
periphery. In this way, the state of Pure Rest becomes
manifested.

Pure Rest is a condition free from the movement of
consciousness, though the Presence is still experienced
on the periphery. What does it mean that the Presence
is experienced on the periphery? How do we know that
it is on the periphery? Because the motionlessness of
Pure Rest is present simultaneously. What is the actual
experience of Pure Rest or motionlessness? The
absence of any modification of consciousness is present
as unconditioned calmness. It is very mysterious, for the
state of Pure Rest belongs neither to the Presence nor
to the Absolute. It is something in-between, a new
dimension of the meeting of the Presence and the
Absolute. This new dimension displays the quality of
both states: it is present as an actual utmostly subtle
experience and is "absent" as existing prior to any
recognition, any experience.

As we already have mentioned, the Absolute State
can be present with or without recognition. The
realization without recognition allows us neither to

understand nor to appreciate the state. To be in this state without the recognition means that the intelligence, together with the underlying presence is registering only the modifications of consciousness. When the sensitivity and intelligence are not fully mature, the state of Absence or Pure Rest is simply not registered. This is the negative "no-mind." The recognition of the Absolute State can take place only when one is sensitive enough to sense and differentiate that which is on the edge of the two realities, beyond consciousness and its absence. All is related to the economy of attention which can be aware of everything that is happening in the field of conscious experience, and at the same time be fully present in the knowingness of Pure Rest.

In the Absolute State, the non-presence of the timeless and the presence of consciousness create one dynamic whole. The intelligence that somehow operates between these two, allows one to participate in the dynamic aspect, while being able to recognize and dwell within the passive, non-active aspect. This recognition is directly connected with a feeling of ease and absolute rest. The recognition feels, discriminates, knows and is. The depth of the Absolute State becomes one with the clarity of intelligence and sensitivity of knowingness.

As we have already mentioned, no tradition from the past clarified that the Ultimate and its recognition are two different things. They did not see that Enlightenment is an event occurring in time and is a fruit of evolution. Enlightenment is like a light entering the darkness of the timeless state. We not only discover that "which is," but we actually add something totally new. This new quality is the secret behind the notion of "recognition." We need to see clearly that it is the recognition that brings into the knowingness, the Ultimate.

At this point the important question to ask is: Who is doing the recognizing? What is <u>that</u> which recognizes the Absolute? The traditional answers that come from the discovery of an empty aspect of the original state are: "nobody," "impersonal consciousness," or "the state is self-recognizing." Although these answers are very sophisticated and profound, they indicate that the awakening to "that one" who recognizes the Absolute and all other states has not yet happened. That which recognizes all states is not merely consciousness, although certainly it is using the tool of consciousness. We will return to this discovery in the chapter about our True Identity. Now we will say only that it is Me in its purest sense, completely personal, intimate and direct, which through wisdom, sensitivity and attention, gives rise to the recognition.

Here we would like to focus on the issue of what the recognition of the Absolute actually is. It is tremendously subtle, for it takes us to the dimension in which we encounter our own absence without losing the quality of being fully conscious. The traditional concept of samadhi sees the realization of the Source as the temporary annihilation of one's consciousness to the point that one forgets one exists. This has no spiritual value and has nothing to do with Enlightenment. To be conscious while absent, to be in a deep sleep state while awake is to be in the Exalted state.

In the act of recognition, we do not simply see our absence. The absence can never become an object of experience. It is the absence that sees us and embraces our being. We do not experience our absence; we experience the absence, the unmanifested, embracing us. This is the dimension of meeting, the divine marriage between the Presence and the Absolute. It is beyond the Presence and beyond the Absolute. It is not just present and it is not just absent. It is not just conscious and it is not just not-aware. It is the Meeting Point. The essence of an Enlightened sage. It is felt as an absolute Pure Rest, free from any movement of consciousness or modifications of elements. A liberation from existence, infinite ease and relief, a Final Peace.

How can the inner attention function between the shores of rest and motionlessness, and the one of activity and psychological movement? It is an important question which can free us from quite popular simplistic and static conclusions. The inner state is very rich and dynamic. The inner attention is like a space containing the movements of mind and feelings, the fluctuation of the state of Presence, the activity in external reality, and at the same time, the dimension of Absolute Rest and absence. This attention can focus more readily on some of these areas, and less on other areas. This attention, being completely effortless and relaxed, is at the same time one with that which we call personal will. The attention cannot be separated from will.

One can, for example, choose, to be absorbed in thoughts and feelings, or to surrender and rest in the Absolute State. But we should not forget that we are in the dimension of wholeness, and although the inner attention can go to different areas, still all is contained in the Absolute State. Even if one is absorbed in the activity of the mind, the attention is at all times completely linked with the Absolute State. It is all about the economy of attention within the state that has merged with the non-attention. Of course the quality of Rest within the Absolute changes if the attention goes out, from the quality of resting exclusively in the Inner. But this is completely natural.

To rest only in the Absolute is a limitation for many, who in the name of self-realization cut off their connection with the manifestation. This is a man-made disidentification. The natural, balanced disidentification is all-inclusive and transcends the attachment to the Absolute. The Absolute State is not apart from all of life. It is the essence, the foundation of life, and that's why it allows all to exist within itself. The recognition, the Enlightened Perception, sees all, for it is a combination of intelligence, sensitivity, clarity and of course, self-realization. The recognition is a flowering of the Source itself, a mirror in which the Unborn can see its timeless face.

The True Meaning of Emptiness

The notion of "Emptiness" is particular popularly in Buddhism. Buddha himself spoke about Emptiness as the nature of reality and the basic characteristic of the Ultimate. It seems important to clarify the real meaning of this concept. Many seek the "literal" experience of Emptiness without the full knowledge of what this term is pointing to. It is a fundamental challenge of all Enlightened beings, that to give a description of the inner reality, one must operate within the limitations of the given vocabulary and language. For this reason, in order to comprehend what Buddha meant by Emptiness, we need to remove all of that which is commonly associated with this word.

What is empty? Is Emptiness an object to be seen? Is it the scientific discovery that the material universe is fundamentally empty, as a form of energy? Is it the true meaning of Emptiness? Or perhaps it means that there is no substance behind our mind and personality? Is the experience of Emptiness a perception of illusory nature of our ego? Is it the experience of bliss or thoughtless awareness in meditation?

All of these areas of experience and perception are not Emptiness. Emptiness is not the experienced or the seen. Neither is Emptiness the perceiver, which is Me. Emptiness is not the state of Presence, which is an energetic experience. Emptiness is "the place" from which the seeing arises: the Absolute.

The "experience" of Emptiness is not an ordinary

experience. It is the ultimate experience which is beyond an experience of "the experienced." To experience Emptiness is to be in the Absolute State. In the Absolute State, the Being aspect of I Am is placed prior to consciousness, that is, prior to experience. In this state, one's being is dropped to the dimension of non-abiding, which is the origin. Here one sees reality from the place which gives rise to the seeing. To experience Emptiness is to rest in it. In this rest one is free, but that freedom is not an object.

Emptiness is not what one is, neither is Emptiness the I Am. Emptiness is where we originate from, and come into the Now, and where the I Am originates from, and comes into the Now. The realization of Emptiness has a very mysterious and subtle nature. This is the reason it is so difficult to describe it. But it is not impossible, that's why we do speak about it.

Emptiness cannot be seen or grasped; but its invisible hands sustain the whole of the Universe and the "I Am".

Mystical State

It is important to know that apart from the Witnessing Consciousness and the Absolute State, there is a possibility of a third state: the mystical state. The mystical state is somewhere between the state of Presence and the Absolute State. Many get stuck on this level of realization unless they receive proper guidance. In the mystical state, the Presence is no longer experienced in a solidified way but one still is not resting in the Absolute. One is in-between, as if suspended, like a leaf floating above the mountain and unable to land.

In reality there are many different kinds of mystical states. Even prior to the realization of the state of Presence, some people experience a variation of the mystical state. What this means is that their Me already has a certain amount of Presence, though it is not solid and has a quality of being "spaced out." Yet it is not fully unconscious of itself either. Here, the person is fluctuating in a partial energy experience of the state of Presence while his/her center is not solidified either in ignorance or in Presence.

Many of these who seek energy states, or don't believe in practicing Presence, live in this reality in satisfaction. The positive aspect of the mystical state is that it gives the person a temporary energetic suspension or freedom from being one's "normal" identity (similar to the effect of drugs). The negative aspects are the seduction of getting stuck in this dimension, for it gives a feeling of freedom, and the fact that this state has no "real" strength to transcend the unconscious mind. In truth, the one in the mystical state can never have a "real" center (Presence). Someone who is simply spaced out is closer to the no-mind experience than the state of Presence. The mystical state or state of being spaced out does not give us the experience of clear Rest and wholeness of being. These experiences lack clarity.

Oneness and Non-separation

Many of us deeply desire to experience the Oneness of the reality we are living in. How can it be possible? What is this Oneness? The relative, limited subject wants to become one with all that is around... Can the Oneness be experienced at all? We can not really talk about the experience of Oneness unless we know what Non-separation is. While the experience of Oneness is *externally* oriented, Non-separation points to the subject.

Before we create an attitude toward objective reality, we should investigate who the perceiver actually is. There is no other way than to start, as always, with the question—Who am I? The observer desires Oneness, but who is this observer? This should be questioned first. We have many opinions about the external reality while taking ourselves for granted, but who is the one who knows? Trying to pinpoint it, we can not find anything substantial. The subject is only a function. What is behind that function? That's what the spiritual search is all about.

The subject is a function, but a function that can relate to itself. When it relates to itself, the feeling of being separated from the rest of reality is born. The subject is a function that has, at the same time, a quality of being at the center. It is the center of becoming. It is not the center of being. To go beyond separation, we need to dispel the illusion that the observer is in the center of being. This illusion can be dispelled only through the positive knowledge of that which we really are. When the illusion that the relative subject is our being drops off, we fall into a deeper place beyond subject/object relationship. That place is a new realm of subjectivity, free from the movement of thoughts.

As long as there is a subject that can relate to itself, that is, to see itself as an object—there is separation. The fundamental reason for the experience of separation is not *how* the person perceives the reality, but the fact that it sees itself as *something*. The moment we shift to the state of consciousness which just is, all is seen as it is. All is seen from the non-modifying perspective. Sometimes we call it Oneness but it is more accurate to identified it as the state of Non-separation. Non-separation is not an experience but the lack of experience of separation. It is not-knowing. Non-separation is always there, it is timeless.

The experience of Oneness, in truth, is born in time. It is a feeling-understanding-perception of the Totality as being contained in this infinite isness of what I am. All is One, but the experience of oneness arises in time and disappears in time—it is not absolute. We can hardly talk about an actual experience of Oneness. It is more like a complete Openness to the Mystery. In that Openness, the all-embracing Wonder is received as our own Presence.

Oneness and Non-separation are the two fundamental aspects of our totality. Non-separation is our foundation--we rest in it eternally, timelessly. Oneness is experienced at the moment when we, as Pure Presence, through the channel of personality, embrace the manifested Existence in the feeling-perception of all-inclusive unity. This feeling cannot be experienced continuously because the relative consciousness, which is responsible for it, becomes tired. At the moment it becomes tired or withdraws its attention from the manifested, all

returns to the state of Non-separation. The state of
Non-separation is effortless and independent from the
relative consciousness. This is our home ground—the
realm beyond knowing and beyond experience.

The feeling of Oneness can be experienced only if
the center of our being is non-abiding, that is, when we
are placed nowhere. That which is having this
experience is the manifested consciousness, expressed
as a personality. This personality can feel the Oneness
because it can feel the separation as well. In itself, it
operates in the realm of separation, but because it is
witnessed by the Absolute, it feels embraced from the
Beyond. In this embrace it knows Oneness.

There are several ways of experiencing Oneness. The
most common is the unconscious Oneness. When a
person is very absorbed in an object or an event, one
forgets about oneself, that is, does not relate to oneself
for a moment. In that instant one doesn't know that
one exists in oneself and therefore does not feel
separated. The subject loses itself in the object. Artists
or people with very empathetic feeling nature often
have these experiences.

A deeper level of Oneness arises when the Witnessing
Consciousness is awakened. The center of identity
shifts from the relative subject (oneself), to the
transcendental state of Presence. The person still
remains, but is witnessed—one loses the illusion of being
in the center. In that state, the polarity subject/object
is penetrated by the all-inclusive light of
Consciousness shining from the background. Although
it is Oneness, it is not total Oneness. It is the Oneness
of manifestation, in the manifestation. The Witnessing
Consciousness, as we know, is not the Ultimate
Subjectivity, though it has qualities that resemble it.
The state of Presence cannot embrace complete

Oneness, for it is not able to remain unmoved. Consciousness by its nature cannot fully rest. One could say that the Witnessing Consciousness allows us to experience the Oneness in the realm of Becoming. In this case it is Conscious Oneness.

The final or total Oneness, which is properly called Non-separation, presents itself when Absolute Subjectivity dissolves the central position of the Witnessing Consciousness. As long as there is any center, the Totality cannot be embraced. In the final shift, our being falls to the Primordial Void, which is Nowhere. It is not just nothing, in the ordinary sense. It truly is, although it can not be experienced. It has only one attribute—it is. Only from that place can we talk about Oneness. And even then we need to remember that this Oneness is far beyond any kind of *experience* of Oneness. The experience of Oneness is only a timely expression of that transcendental, timeless Oneness that—purely Is.

II

Realm of the Human

Being Human

Being human is to feel deeply the paradox of being alive. We cannot just live spontaneously like plants and animals. We are too conscious of the contradictions of life! Our understanding and sensitivity are constantly being challenged by the "resistance" of the outer reality. Our greatest challenge is that we are not just *given*— we have to create ourselves. We are becoming. A human being is not an entity, but a flow of intelligence, a process of self-creation. Apart from living in the practical, objective world, we live in a *theoretical*, conceptual reality. We not only live in the world—we also think about the world. Our theoretical reality is constantly confronting and being confronted by the reality of our direct experiences.

Our thoughts have a tremendous impact on the objective world; they give us great manipulative power— we can transform the world, as well as destroy it. That is the potential, and the dangerous side of our mind. On the other hand, our mind is constantly being affected and shaped by objective reality. What we think and feel has been largely conditioned by the physical and cultural environment. We and the world co-create each other in the dance of living. This is the dynamic between the subjective and objective polarities of existence. <u>We live in the world and the world is inside our own heads</u>. Our theoretical reality distances us from the process of living; and we feel acutely separated from existence. We strongly experience the world as being *outside*. This psychologically difficult situation in which we are deprived of feeling united with life, however, gives us the potential to go beyond not only conscious separation, but also unconscious oneness. We left animal kingdom, which is the unconscious ignorance, to evolve through our present conscious ignorance into the conscious awakening.

Apart from relating to the external world, we have the capacity of reflecting upon ourselves—to create an ego-image. We have a strong need to assert ourselves, to give acknowledgment to our image, so that we feel acceptable in our own judgment. This is done usually in a mechanical and unconscious way. This checking has an extremely strong emotional impact, for one is fully identified with the ego-image. Because one doesn't know anything else, the ego-image is one's only trace of identity and the only source of power and security in the world.

We should not forget that the ability to create a self-image, though having ego limiting connotations, also has a very important role in our personal evolution and development. In the process of self-creating, we need to grow in many areas—in the physical, emotional, inter-personal and spiritual. Deep down we are growing to fulfill the vision of our Soul, which wants to express itself in this reality in a unique way. Harmony, love and spiritual understanding are the general, fundamental principles behind the desire to grow.

When we are born, the deep sensitivity of our Soul meets this insensitive world. No wonder there is so much pain in our heart! The little child, thrown into cruel reality, has to strive to survive, psychologically and physically...isn't it sad? From the beginning we are told what and how we should be. The particular, socially accepted ego-image is imposed upon us by our parents and society, usually with "good" intentions. They operate from the standpoint of collective human consciousness and their own personal experiences. We have no other choice but to learn from what humanity and our surroundings have to offer us. On the other hand, we absolutely need to find our own understanding and retain our own unique sensitivity. In the process of self-creating, one learns from a wide variety of experiences, from our human cultural inheritance, to the striving to assert one's unique sensitivity, perception and understanding of reality.

There are two basic polarities in our internal life. One relates to all our idealistic tendencies and desires. And the second–to the realistic, survival and practical aspects of our life. One we could call "idealism," and the other, "realism." If we look deeper into our idealistic tendencies, while removing all shallow conditionings linked to them, we get close to an area of extremely deep existential sensitivity. The desire for love, harmony, compassion, kindness and beauty are the basic qualities, the blueprints of our soul. They are directly connected with our divine, universal inheritance. Our morality is only a pale and distorted reflection of that truth.

But human life is a paradox. The deepest aspirations of our soul are confronted with the biological and psychological restrictions of the world we happen to be living in. And however we interpret it–this is Reality, it is the Truth. The Truth is beyond idealism and realism as well. Truth is a paradox! In creating ourselves we constantly strive to harmonize the desires and wishes of our heart with a realistic perspective on reality. Whatever our ideas about life are—life is more than those ideas. Life is our challenge.

The religious ideal is to renounce some part of our human nature in order to escape from the paradox. It is theoretically possible. One can repress natural desires and tendencies in the name of spiritual idealism. Spiritual idealism has given rise to the institution of the "holy man." It is a symbol or an archetype of that ancient longing for an escape from living in the contradiction—in-between the extremes of idealism and realism. But we need to see reality as it is, if we want to live in the Truth. Our desire for love and harmony is the truth, as well as the contradictions of life, the imperfection of our human nature, our emotional vulnerability and our needs in many areas—all of this is the truth. This should not be judged. The religious judgments went very deep into our psyche, provoking feelings of guilt. They were created from a place without compassion. We must have compassion for our human nature, because it is a part of the whole truth.

Human life is about bringing balance and harmony into the contradictions we must face. Nothing is to be discarded; all is valid, all has its place. We are learning how not to eliminate parts of our human nature, such as desires or conflicting emotions, but to develop wisdom and understanding within their existence. This is where the journey toward compassion begins.

Free Will

As we go into higher levels of abstraction, we encounter a higher degree of complexity. There are those times when the mind is taken away by its desire to comprehend reality and somehow loses contact with this very reality. The moment, for example, we try to look at ourselves from the perspective of All-Embracing Consciousness, it is difficult to find a place for an individual. If all is God, if all is Emptiness, if all is Consciousness, how can we talk about individuality and free will at all?

Transcendental logic however, goes beyond this way of thinking. When we understand that the individual is not a static entity separated from the flow of life, but rather, a unique expression of that flow itself, we have insight into the Paradox.

Understanding is a unity of an idea and reality. When the weight of the idea is heavier than reality, we go astray from the alive truth. The Paradox is: it is alive. Transcendental logic appears when the highest conceptual insight into the nature of reality meets the factual experience of *what is* and these two melt into the Paradox. To truly see the Paradox is only possible from the non-conceptual state. Unless the Paradox is embraced in the space of allowance, it can not be contained.

The truth is absolutely present. There is not a shadow of a doubt. All questions are alive as the answers— within the Paradox. Transcendental logic allows everything to be, beyond comprehension. Although there is certainly no place for the individual in this vast totality, still there is a place to be an individual. That being an individual is theoretically impossible and practically possible is the Paradox. When the possible and impossible meet, transcendental logic embraces it—*as such.*

What is free will? What is the will? Will is life. It is the force to be, to create, to manifest...Will is Time. The flow of Time is the will. This is the foundation.

What is free? When the cause turns into the effect, it is a matter of law; the effect is determined–there is no question of being free or not free here. There is only one area where free will could possibly apply—the area of making decisions. If we look at the individual from the external perspective, as the result of collective consciousness, the environment and its own past—we can hardly conceive that there is a possibility of free will. Only by seeing that the Universal Intelligence, the source of Existence, creates us from Within, can we sense the mystery of free will present as a Paradox. That which we are is the Mystery being experienced from within. The divine light of intelligence operating within us is rooted in the unknown. Within our conditioned and limited mind is the *Unpredictable.* We are the past exploding into the Now. This explosion, within all limitations, is Free.

The Role of Ego

In most spiritual traditions, the role of the ego-personality in the process of reaching Enlightenment is, to a great extent underestimated and misunderstood. Unless we see clearly that the ego in itself is something absolutely positive and, as such, the only tool for arriving at higher levels of awareness, we have no way to understand the process of awakening.

Many seekers are confused and not able to comprehend the apparent paradox of transcending the ego without actually annihilating it. In Buddhist psychology, there is a concept that ego is not real, for it is only a play of so called five skandhas. This concept is missing the elemental understanding that our body-mind operates as an alive and coherent organism of intelligence in a purposeful and meaningful way. The ego cannot be found anywhere as such, for the one looking for it—is the ego. It is too close to be found, but certainly it is always there.

It is difficult to define what the ego is, for it is not anything substantial. We would define ego as a self-conscious function of individualized consciousness capable of relating to its surroundings and itself in a centralized and intelligent manner. The ego is not an entity, but rather a unified field of identity—it is not fixated on a point, but operates within a spatial consciousness. It has many layers and many aspects.

In Buddhist tradition there's a concept of "no-mind," and so we tend to think that our being is simply divided into the mind and the no-mind. This is far too simplistic. Even when we go beyond the gross level of thinking, the mind is still functioning and the ability for self-relating is retained. This thing called ego is constantly accompanying the process of meditation and, allows us to create clarity and understanding. The art of resting within the stillness of our being, and the self-conscious movement of our intelligence are not separated from one another. Without the gentle checking of our state during meditation and cultivation in general, we would be unable to make any progress in the practice. This is the function of the ego.

Now, before going deeper into the issue of how the ego and enlightened state relate to one another, we need to understand what Enlightenment is. True Enlightenment has nothing to do with any modification or transformation of the ego-personality in terms of eliminating desires, negative emotions or developing positive qualities. Neither does it involve seeing into the "non-existence" or "emptiness" of the ego. Any "seeing" or conceptual understanding is confined only to the relative functions of our intelligence. The state of Enlightenment is truly a new dimension of being, beyond the realm of personality.

Most traditions refer to Enlightenment as an awakening and permanent abiding in the state of "thoughtless awareness," also called "rigpa," "witnessing consciousness" or "presence." Complete Enlightenment however goes deeper into the nature of reality. Even the state of Presence, which represents consciousness in its purest form, belongs to the realm of experience, that is, to the realm of time. The final Enlightenment takes us to the place of Pure Rest in the non-abiding ground of all existence, which is beyond awareness and its modifications. This is what the Unborn is.

The ego-personality not only participates and promotes the shift of our being into the deeper dimensions of reality, from the state of Presence to resting in the Absolute, but it also allows us to comprehend our post-Enlightenment situation. Enlightenment is not the end of our growth. The understanding of the Enlightened state and its relation to the ego as well as to the manifested reality is constantly evolving. The ego and Enlightened state co-exist in a very interesting way—*they relate to each other.*

In the case of the non-awakened person, there is total identification with the functioning of the mind. One is living in a semi-conscious, dreamlike state. This is called the darkness of ignorance. After awakening, the thought process is no longer in the center of our being; one abides in the unconditioned stillness of the original state. But we should not forgot that at the same time, the self-conscious intelligence can and does relate back to that stillness. For example, how the ego relates to the Essence results in various stages of absorption. Even after realization, the ego and our Essence are in a very rich and dynamic relationship—they are simultaneously present.

Those masters who claim that they have no ego, prove to have a certain psychological ignorance; or there're using the term in an improper way. They are most likely victims of certain idealistic, linear and simplistic spiritual logic. The transcendental logic embracing the apparent paradox (the co-existence of the ego and the egoless state), goes beyond this simple logic in the apperception of the truth which is not conceptual but alive.

The goal and purpose of Enlightenment is not to eliminate the ego, but to enlighten it. How could we possibly enlighten it if we deny its very existence? To enlighten the ego is to create within the personal intelligence a clear understanding that our personality, with all its limitations, and our timeless essence, is an indivisible, dynamic whole. It is here that the humility, intelligence and the highest spiritual realization meet. Ego, the operative center of our personality, even after melting with the Source, must face this never-ending challenge of fulfilling the dynamic balance between its participation in the manifested reality and of resting in the Absolute. The absolute dimension and human perspective are truly one. But although they are one, they give birth to one another in the continuous process of arriving at wholeness.

The Fifth Noble Truth:
The Purpose of Suffering

When Buddha Shakhyamuni described the "Four Noble Truths," his main concern was to reveal the painful aspect of Existence and to show the way of liberation from it. It was absolutely sufficient in his times, for even the message of freedom from the relative phenomenal reality was extremely difficult to be grasped. However, the evolution of human consciousness continues, and although we live in a very complex world, our capacity to comprehend the mystery of Existence and our role in it has greatly increased. In our evolution, we are continuously transcending the human linear logic, coming closer and closer to the transcendental logic of Life itself, to the understanding that is embraced in the wisdom of Totality. The "Fifth Noble Truth" points to a higher perspective of viewing the problem of suffering, beyond the dualism of suffering and the end of suffering. It complements the "Four Noble Truths," containing them in a more complete vision.

Before we talk about the "Fifth Noble Truth" we need to see clearly what is meant by the notion "the end of suffering," which is the essence of the "Four Noble Truths." It is absolutely wrong to assume that Enlightenment *destroys* suffering. Suffering cannot be destroyed, for it is simply part of Life. Buddha knew it and that's why he found that the only way to "end" suffering was to go beyond existence itself. Where is that mysterious "place" of the Beyond? It is a life riddle for all of those who are in search of freedom. That which is Beyond, that which is Free in itself cannot be found in the realm of space and time, cannot become an object of experience—but certainly it is and it can be realized. The timeless, non-abiding Essence that gives rise to the totality of manifestation is truly our own innate nature, and the awakening *unites* it with the conscious mind of an individual. Enlightenment does not end the suffering—it is *that* to which one is enlightened that is the "end" of suffering or more properly speaking: it is the "non-suffering" itself. What this means is that we do not eliminate suffering but rather add the dimension of non-suffering. Enlightenment is not about negation but about expansion. This needs to be clearly understood.

We can speak about the pre-Enlightenment and post-Enlightenment experience of suffering. Prior to Enlightenment, not knowing our true nature, we are completely identified with the phenomenal aspect of our being, which results in excessive suffering, which is ignorance. After Enlightenment the Unmanifested Essence of our totality becomes awakened—the sphere of non-suffering, the final peace and freedom. But that is not all. Enlightenment is not just about liberation—it is about completion. Buddha, the Awakened One is not only the Unborn, the "not coming, not going, not staying;" he/she is also a human being, a part of the universal flow of life in its eternal journey in time. Even if the Enlightenment to the Unborn has been completed, the Enlightenment to Totality is happening eternally as the inherent function of the Now.

In the realm of ignorance, suffering calls for liberation. In the realm of Enlightenment, suffering is seen as a part of Totality, a necessary element of the ecological system of Existence. It is because of suffering that its opposites: joy, happiness and beauty can be experienced. Suffering can be seen as an indivisible part of that energy through which our evolution, growth and expansion happens. Liberation is not the purpose but a tool, by which we can aim at completion. In this completion, suffering is not annihilated but embraced in a wider, holistic perspective. The sky of Enlightenment is completely one with the clouds of suffering and the wind of bliss. Nothing is excluded in the apperception of Totality. The Enlightenment is so profound because it is in absolute alignment with the wisdom of all-embracing Totality. In the Enlightened vision there is still a place for individual imperfection and suffering. It is a paradox that cannot be grasped by the linear mind. The Awakened One is not just a liberated being. Buddha Mind is a realm of pure perception, pure experience and pure Rest, where the Primordial, the Unconditioned, the Unborn is the very life of human personality, which certainly includes suffering.

The "Fifth Noble Truth" has been introduced to take us beyond an over simplistic understanding of Enlightenment and its relation to our human life in regards to the problem of suffering. Existence *is not* our enemy, and the suffering that is an integral part of life has, without a shadow of a doubt, an important purpose and function in our evolution as well as in the evolution of the Universe. The purpose of suffering cannot be explained in simple terms—it has to be apperceived from the timeless place of silence, from the place where *I am not.*

At this point we discover the deeper meaning of Suchness. Suchness is not just a cool, thoughtless and detached perception of reality. True Suchness is an apperception of the Totality in which our absence, sensitivity, wisdom and the warm fullness of empathy become completely the Now. Enlightenment goes beyond the liberating aspects of self-realization, that is, beyond the attainment of the "end of suffering." In this act of "going beyond," life, for the first time, is experienced in its wholeness. It is neither the suffering nor the end of it that is the whole truth. The Truth is a paradox operating within the non-linear intelligence of Life. In this understanding we see clearly the mysterious and profound wisdom behind the experience of suffering.

The purpose of suffering is its very experience; this experience points to the Now and the Now points back to the Mystery. In the process of spiritual awakening we certainly extinguish the *unnecessary* suffering that is a product of conditioned, neurotic mind, but even then, the *natural* suffering always remains as a part of a wide variety of human experiences. To arrive truly at the complete, non-dualistic and whole Vision of reality, not only suffering has to be transcended but liberation as well. The complete human is beyond suffering and liberation–because of this, he/she is one with the Mystery, which is the totality of the Now.

Misconceptions About Enlightenment

Enlightenment is a gateless gate to the final peace beyond becoming. This tremendous insight into the nature of reality is certainly rare. People who have reached "it" are treated with enormous respect and admiration and are called masters and Buddhas. Unfortunately, in the eyes of certain people and some spiritual "poets," the vision of Enlightenment grew to a size far beyond its reality, which certainly has nothing to do with common sense.

When we don't achieve the experience of something that we deeply desire, our imagination and expectations tend to outgrow the form of its reality. No wonder that that is the case for *Great Enlightenment*; it is extremely difficult to set the borders between our projections and the factual situation. That's why our vision of Enlightenment has become too big to be attained, too big to be conceived and too big to have any reflection in our everyday life. In addition, often spiritual teachers seem to be very happy to use the situation which can be described as "I know and you don't," for promoting their own self-image and making Enlightenment even more vague and mysterious. Unless humility is attained, the spiritual teacher is immature.

We would like to clarify certain misunderstandings and prejudices evolving around the magical notion of Enlightenment. The meaning of Self-realization is indeed profound but at the same time simple and ordinary. We have been talking about what Enlightenment is. It is now time to make clear "What it is not."

1. Enlightenment does not annihilate the ego. Why would someone want to annihilate something so useful and extraordinary? It has not been by chance that we have mentioned many times how important the mind and ego are as the creative force of our intelligence. We need to dissolve this dangerous spiritual conditioning that has taken deep root in our habitual way of thinking. Irresponsible psychological language has caused a lot of harm to those on the Path. The ego concept needs to be defined in a way that relates to our everyday experience, and to all those complicated processes in meditation and on the spiritual Path.

In the case of people without insight into the nature of consciousness, the mental activity is in the center of consciousness. Every thought creates a new center, a new identification which is the ego–there is nothing else there. We cannot talk about "one" ego but rather about a flow of conscious or semi-conscious events, being capable of operating in a relatively integrated way. This is the function of the ego.

When Enlightenment takes place, the Presence becomes the center, and there is the feeling that all the thoughts are only witnessed objects-events on the periphery of consciousness; they are guests coming and going, having nothing to do with the stillness of our being. For that reason, it is easy to conclude that there is only Witnessing, and the rest is irrelevant, impersonal and objective. But this popular conclusion is one-dimensional and is not able to grasp the dynamics of human consciousness. Thoughts are being witnessed and observed. The center is empty and uninvolved. Is that all? Not fully. Although the thoughts are witnessed, the intelligence which is using them represents also a parallel center of relative consciousness-it is also the "Me."

We can speak about two centers within us, as manifested beings: one is the Witnessing Consciousness—a constant flow of presence, and the second is the moving self-conscious center of our personality. When we see this clearly, there is no doubt that the thoughts, which are being witnessed, are simultaneously an indivisible part of Me, and it is Me who is thinking them! In the case of an Enlightened being, although thoughts have a different quality, still they remain as a function of consciousness and as a functional self-relating center, which we interpret as "me." The absolute Me and the relative me are one. Being and self-conscious expression are one.

The ego concept refers not only to the gross level of thinking or to the gross will. We have already spoken about the fact that to divide our consciousness into thinking and not-thinking is far too simplistic. Consciousness is extraordinarily rich. There is intuitive knowing, feeling, gentle checking and being attentive to what is happening in our consciousness and surroundings. This movement of intelligence has a quality of self-referral which is also what we call–the ego. The personality without Presence is ignorance of course, but Presence without the personality is like a tree without fruit, the sun without rays or a flower without fragrance. They are one organic whole. When we fully understand that ego is "good," the whole issue of eliminating it drops off by itself. But this is not yet the end. We are coming now to the next complicated problem: what kind of ego should we have?

2. Enlightenment does not destroy all that is traditionally considered as negative in our personality. It is not easy to be a human being, to live with the conflicts and contradictions of our human nature. That's why it doesn't surprise us that the highest of human attainments, Enlightenment, is directly associated with getting rid of all that is disturbing our peaceful living. What kind of feelings are we allowed to feel if we want to be *spiritual?* Which desires are we allowed to have? How should we behave in order to be like the Enlightened supermen? In the spiritual field there is a lot of judgment about how one should be, and unfortunately, most are coming from the desire to negate our human nature. Beginning the spiritual journey, one is often given a model describing which parts of our personality should be regarded as negative and which positive. But can we really say what is negative? It is pretty easy to put aside a wide spectrum of conflicting feelings and emotions by classifying them as defilement and ignorance-but by doing so, we suddenly lose a natural perspective of our life as human beings. Can we really say, that emotions of anger, fear, restlessness or boredom are negative by nature? Can we not find wisdom behind them? Aren't they an important part of life itself?

One feels embarrassed reading all the descriptions about the perfect "Awakened One." Most are inhuman or simply ignorant. Unfortunately, in the pseudo-spiritual consciousness, all that is related to challenge and suffering is negated, while all that is sweet, loving and peaceful becomes the ideal? How can we eliminate some of our feelings and leave the others? It is simply not possible! There is no life without desire, fear and anger. Without them we would have died a long time ago! These feelings carry the wisdom of life and allow us to survive in the ecological organism of existence.

3. Many associate enlightenment with desirelessness.
Isn't it unbelievable? How many seekers on the Path are
misled by wrong views like this! Without desires how
could one live? It is life that desires life. We live, for we
are an expression of this basic desire. We can reach the
Ultimate only because we *desired* it–there is no doubt
about that. We can be sure that reaching the Ultimate
has nothing to do with being desireless–it is a new
dimension of consciousness and not just an empty
space that remains after annihilating human nature.
Buddha doesn't become a Buddha because he/she has
dissolved attachment and all sorts of disturbing
tendencies–although that might be an outcome. His/
her state is beyond. It is our nature, whether we are
holy or unholy.

Without fear one would be killed by the car the very
first day on the street. How often anger helps us to get
out of difficult situations? What a powerful energy it is!
If someone, in the name of spiritual ideas, wishes to
renounce desire and choose death–there is no judgment,
but let's not forget that it has nothing to do with the
phenomena of Self-realization. We need to be honest
about reality. There is no human being who does not
experience feelings of desire, anger, fear, impatience...
But along comes a religious leader with authority who
condemns these feelings as standing in the way to
heaven or Enlightenment.

In reality, it is not about what kind of feelings or
emotions we experience, but rather why they arise and
what we do with them. We are learning throughout life,
how to live in harmony with our inherent tendencies
and predispositions. There is no need to eliminate
anything as such. All these feelings and emotions are

an extension of our being, and it is only due to them
that we are able to face the challenge of life. The only
thing that needs to be transformed is our unconscious
mind and emotional immaturity. Our emotional
inheritance must be imbibed with intelligence, sensitivity
and wisdom. This is the way. Enlightenment allows us
to see our personality from the place of silence and
natural aloofness of pure consciousness. From that
perspective, we can become really human.

**4. Enlightenment does not end the process of learning
and growing.** It is very important to understand that
even after completing our inner journey and gaining
the final peace, on the personal level we are always
beginners. There is no end to our emotional
development and the deepening of our sensitivity.
There is no end to gaining understanding of life and
the Universe we are living in. Learning is Life. We can
say that Enlightenment in the realm of Being is finite,
but the Enlightenment in the realm of Becoming is
never ending.

**5. A perfect state of Presence does not necessarily
manifest itself as perfect action.** Is Enlightened being
always responding in an appropriate manner to the
challenges of the moment because his consciousness is
in the state of perfect clarity? In many meditation
schools, one practices mindfulness of the environment,
which is a tool to connect the practitioner with empirical
time. It is the Presence however, which is the witnessing
of empirical time. One can be perfectly aware of the
environment without being in the Presence. Being
present and being in the Presence are not the same.
When we are aware of this, we no longer identify
mindfulness of the object with the Presence itself. The

action is never perfect, for it belongs to the relative consciousness. The relative consciousness is there, not to be pedantically meticulous but, very importantly, to be sufficient in the process of living.

We could say that it is as if there are two awakenings: one is to the perfection of our eternal essence— remote, free and everlasting. Second, to the imperfection of our human nature. Here imperfection doesn't mean that something is wrong—it is the nature of becoming that the ideal can not be reached. In this dimension of evolution we are not seeking perfection but for balance and harmony within the polarities.

6. Enlightenment does not necessarily results in extraordinary psychic powers. What does Awakened One see, hear and know? What supernatural powers does he have? Does he see all? Does he know all? Is his power absolute? These rather embarrassing questions have been the subject of serious investigation for many Buddhist and non-Buddhist thinkers during the last two thousands years. Again, what is responsible for this misunderstanding is a kind of simplistic logic and philosophy. Enlightenment is a realization of the oneness with the source of all manifestation. In Buddhism it is called–One Mind. We may think that the person who unites with the One Mind naturally would have access to the content of the whole manifestation. But this kind of reasoning is quite primitive and indicates a narrow ego point of view.

Unless we grasp the distinction between the Absolute Subjectivity and the relative one, we will not be able to see how the One Mind and the person who has realized it, relate to each other. If the little flower gets awakened to the existence of the whole planet or even the whole Universe, it would still remain a little and delicate plant. The Ultimate Subjectivity has nothing to do with the individual perspective. The question is not about *knowing* something or *having* something as an individual. The opposite is true. Enlightenment is about shifting to the dimension of consciousness that is beyond relative knowledge and relative power, because all knowledge and power are relative. Becoming one with the One is beyond knowing—it is the utmost innocence.

The relative subject is by its nature limited; it is but an angle from which the Totality becomes aware of itself as the manifestation and finally as the Unmanifested—it is necessarily limited. Because of this creative limitation, the Totality can *freeze* the perception and recognize it as Time. Buddha knows all, for he/she knows that all is Consciousness. He is present everywhere for he is the Presence; and he is beyond manifestation for he is beyond Consciousness. Enlightenment is not an acquisition, but rather dissolution of the ego-centered perception of reality. The question is not about knowledge or power; the Enlightened state is purely *beyond.* When one is awakened to be a no-thing, nothing in the Universe can be a hindrance. The Nothing melts with the Nothing—this is the ultimate knowledge and the ultimate power. This is the greatest miracle. Let's not forget that. From this Nothing the true human being can be born, the human being who knows what beauty, love and humility are.

Meditation can open certain psychic channels, awaken kundalini force and develop some unusual abilities. But developing the skill of manipulating energies is not equated with the Enlightened state. These abilities can certainly be developed, but to think that they have anything to do with the Awakening is a serious misunderstanding. The psychic realm, as well as the realm of energy, belongs to the grosser level of reality than the dimension of the Self. This must be seen fully, for this understanding liberates!

We hope that this presentation of what Enlightenment is not has been helpful in understanding the misconceptions about the nature of Self-realization. Now we can see spiritual awakening from a more natural, simple and truly human perspective—a meeting of clarity and compassion.

III

Realm of the Divine

The Pitfall of Enlightenment

Reaching the Absolute can be very dangerous, for there is the possibility of dissolving the Soul. The pull from the bottomless ocean of stillness absorbs all feelings and thoughts into its original Emptiness. It is very easy to get stuck in the experience of Peace. Enlightenment brings the conviction that all has been reached and it is enough to rest in the effortless state of Absolute Stillness. But it is not the end. As we had to use effort to reach the state of Peace, so now we need to move out of it if we wish to reach our Soul. And reaching the Soul is our ultimate task, for she is that which we truly are.

To reach the Soul, we need to allow ourselves again to desire, to feel, to be vulnerable and sensitive. Peace is not completion. We are not here only "not to suffer," this is a mistaken concept. Peace is absolutely important as the foundation from where the expansion must come. And the expansion can occur only through the Heart. In the Emptiness, the diamond needs to be found—the rainbow in our Heart. To move out of the Emptiness, and to the feelings and sensitivity of the Heart is an act of courage and a sign of great spirit.

To motivate one to remove oneself from the Absolute State, the Soul may bring feelings of restlessness and lack of fulfillment. One starts to doubt whether one is fully complete. "Why am I suffering? An Enlightened being is supposed to be in a state free of suffering?! Is there something wrong with my attainment?" It is always the feeling of suffering that brings us to the experience of the Soul. As long as we live in various robes of false identities, we are more or less in the state of suffering. Real liberation is not about exiting this dimension, but finding full completion. Without the awakening of the Soul, we are far from being complete and fulfilled. We succeeded in freeing ourselves from the Manifestation and now the new task arises: <u>to get out of the Unmanifested.</u>

Disidentification

Disidentification has always been the main focus of all traditional teachings on our planet regarding Enlightenment. Because life as such is a form of identification, to disidentify, one needs to choose the unmanifested: that which is prior to existence. If we look more closely at this choice, we can see how strongly it has been conditioned by certain life negating philosophies. The deep longing to find freedom from suffering and to exit the challenge of life in conflicting reality, gave rise to the ideal of renunciation. From the other side, the shift to the Absolute creates a natural pull, a gravitational force towards non-involvement, non-activity and passivity. Compared to the effortless rest in the Absolute, any action in the manifestation seems like an effort. So we can see that behind the ideal of disidentification are two elements. One is the natural quality of the Absolute State with its pull towards the Unmanifested, and the second is the traditional philosophy that has created within the psyche a negative attitude towards the personality and its positive participation in life.

Disidentification represents the movement from ignorance to the Self, to the Source. It is extremely important as a part of the process. One cannot reach the Source unless there is a necessary amount of detachment and freedom from involvement. The energy of life that is continuously moving outward, must be radically turned inward to reach the Source.

It is once again about the economy of energy, the economy of attention. Absolute disidentification cannot exist unless one chooses death. We would rather talk about minimum identification, minimum energy given to the personality and life. Let's call it the minimum ego.

Although disidentification is a valid attitude toward life, it is still partial and incomplete. It is incomplete for it doesn't see all—it chooses negative freedom, to exit from the manifested. Identification, on the other hand, is incomplete because it lacks the freedom of the Beyond: it refers only to the participation; that's why it is just an illusion. Identification negates the Source, the foundation of all being, because it is outside the field of its perception. From the other side, disidentification negates life, the positive expression of the Source; it is also partial. Disidentification is a tool that needs to be used in an intelligent manner; otherwise it will bring us to the verge of "Enlightened" alienation.

In the beginning, we are totally identified with our phenomenal expression. The inherent desire to survive and to attain maximum physical and psychological well being, governs our life. Identification is purely instinctive and unconscious. Unless we are able to step out of our personal reality, we cannot evolve spiritually. To renounce and surrender the personal, so that the higher can be reached is the price for our evolution. To renounce means to take the energy and focus from "doing" and "having" to the realm of "being." The personality doesn't see the state of Being as a direct acquisition—it is conditioned to invest its energy into the dimension of time. That's why disidentification carries in itself the element of renunciation. It is in the economy of evolution that to reach the higher, we need to renounce the lower.

From identification we move to disidentification. From one extreme into another. Who am I in separation from this body and mind? The center of my identity is slowly moving Beyond. The Witnessing Consciousness is being born; the personality is seen as more and more on the periphery. Disidentification at this stage can be perceived as a shift of identification—from the personality to the Presence. The final disidentification takes place when even the Presence is transcended in the Absolute State, in the state without any center or point of identity.

But the personality still exists, with certain desires and needs. How is it possible? We need to understand that the term disidentification points to two areas. One is the nature of reality which ultimately refers to the Absolute State. Second, is a choice made within the personality. Within the personality there is always present an economy of identification, choosing where to participate and where to withdraw one's energy. Between these two shores, the life of personality flows. As far as personality is concerned, the complete disidentification, as we have said, is impossible. What occurs is relative disidentification. Relative disidentification allows a certain amount of energy to be left for the personality's sake, but directs most of the energy toward the Source. When complete disidentification is realized, which is the Absolute State itself, we have an interesting situation: the complete disidentification co-exists with the relative identification. However, at this stage, the weight of being is with the disidentification, as if the relative identification was only a necessary compromise.

From ignorant identification we have moved to Enlightened disidentification, which allows a minimum of identification. Is this the end? If this was the end it would be also the end of evolution! Evolution is much more than the attainment of Buddhahood. Buddhahood is just a beginning; one is like a baby cleansed from ignorance and unconsciousness—life at last in its true sense begins. From Enlightened disidentification, we must take a step towards positive and Enlightened Identification. It is only now that the magical circle can be complete. The Truth is beyond identification and disidentification—it encompasses all of reality. Disidentification is the foundation and identification is its expression. The delicate balance between these two is the art of Being, which can be mastered only by those who have reached the Enlightened state and have transcended it in the act of opening to the beauty of life.

Life is divine, for it comes from the Divine source. To renounce it and disidentify with it fully, is to go against the Divine. So, as one wakes up to the ultimate disidentification, finally one must also wake up to the Enlightened Identification and positive participation in the flow of evolution. How can it be done?

Beyond Enlightenment

The Enlightened state is one of disidentification. There is no center, no focal point, no connection with reality. The only connection with the world can be one of compassion, of Bodhisattva, which is the last excuse to give oneself a reason to live. The ideal of the Bodhisatva can be seen as a compensation, an attempt to avoid one-sided disidentification or negative freedom. Now we leave behind the teachings about Enlightenment. This teaching is directed to those who are already in the Enlightened state. Enlightenment is not the end. What to do with it? How to live? How to evolve and go further?

The wisdom of the Absolute does not allow us to remain in the clinical situation of disidentification. The Absolute must meet the reality of its own Manifestation. The meeting of the Absolute with the Creation can take place only if a new center is opened. It cannot happen in the no-center state. This new center, the place where the Absolute meets the world—is the Heart.

When the Heart center opens, one shifts from the non-abiding of the Absolute to the place where the "non-abiding" and the "abiding in the heart" become one. This place is neither in nor out, neither within nor without, beyond identification and disidentification. Here the two dimensions of seemingly opposite realities meet and for the first time one experiences real wholeness.

Without knowing the Soul, experiencing oneself and

life in general as basically positive are impossible. One can certainly experience the peace and bliss of inner silence; but the heart, the Soul, is still unfulfilled. Compared with the experience of the Soul, the inner Emptiness or thoughtless state is closer to neutral, without flavor, than positive. The experience of happiness and bliss can truly happen only through the Heart. Because one is resting in the Heart, the gravitational pull from the Absolute doesn't bring any more disidentification. There is a perfect balance, which allows one to be at ease in the unmanifested and manifested at the same time. The Heart is the middle point. It transcends the polarity of the Source and Creation for it is directly linked with the Creator. It is only in the Heart that all feels fulfilled and complete.

The awakening of the Heart has nothing to do with the ideals of compassion or of saving others. The Heart is a dimension of its own and serves its own purpose. Our purpose in opening the Heart is not to love others, but to find who we really are. After Enlightenment, our basic identity is dissolved. The personality still functions, but it cannot give us a sense of identity any longer. It is easy at this point, to conclude that there is actually "nobody" here, and everything is empty without the self. But this is not true.

As the dimension of the Absolute needs to be awakened, so does our True Identity. The answer to this identity is in the Heart center. The Absolute enters through the Crown center and dissolves everything until it dissolves itself in the Hara. From the Hara, it needs to return to the Heart to establish the divine balance between the Unmanifested and the World. Without the Heart, one cannot really live, for there is no connection whatsoever with existence. One remains aloof, detached and isolated, missing the experience of life. It is a very dangerous idea that we are here to find liberation. It is much more positive than this.

So we open the Heart center, not to become a Bodhisattva or out of compassion (unless it is the compassion for ourselves first). Compassion at this point, naturally arises based on the inherent wisdom of the Heart. Without the Heart, although we might think that the suffering has been transcended, in truth our Soul is still suffering and longing for herself. Because we have a Soul, even after the realization of the Absolute State, we still remain in the realm of suffering. It is only the awakening of the Heart that brings us to Wholeness. In the Heart, the Absolute meets the manifested and the Creator meets the Soul. The Heart brings warmth to the coolness of the Absolute and brings fullness to the Emptiness of disidentification. It is the only place where we can free ourselves from the powerful pull from the Unmanifested.

As there is an Enlightenment to the Absolute, so there is an Enlightenment to the Heart; a full opening of the Heart center. For many years and many life times we have been suppressing our sensitivity, vulnerability and innocence in order to be strong and reach the Ultimate. Especially on the path of will, one must use very masculine energy which closes the Heart. All of us have been deeply hurt in our childhood, which additionally prevents us from opening our Hearts. There are many elements, but let's remain clear that it is the will of the Divine itself which allows us to open our Heart and to meet its beauty and sensitivity. Because it is the will of the Divine, do we truly have a choice?

The Soul: Our True Identity

Who am I? Am I the Absolute? Am I the pure "I Am"? Am I Consciousness? In the search for our true identity we are moving through different layers and dimensions of our totality. But who are we truly? The Absolute, the Consciousness and the personal self are nothing but different dimensions of what we are. To choose one of these dimensions and say "I am That" would be incorrect and one-sided. We are all of that. We are the mind, the body, the state of Presence and fundamentally the underlying timeless Source. But there is something more. Within all of what we are, there is the heart of our unique identity: the Soul.

Unfortunately, the word "Soul," as well as other similar words like the "Self" or "Higher Self," is commonly used without the experiential understanding of its real meaning. This notion seems to be a sort of a metaphysical excuse to fill up the hole in understanding. For most, it is just an abstract, vague notion giving a feeling of something spiritual, connecting an individual with eternity and God. On the other hand, many New Age thinkers and channels speak about the Soul without having the proper experience and knowledge of the Buddha State. And in reality, only when reflected in the pure mirror of the original state, the Soul can be fully discovered.

It is not true that everybody "has" a Soul. It is a paradox that although everybody is an expression of one's Soul, not everybody "has" a Soul. The Soul in most cases is unconscious, as the "I Am" is. It is like a dim light behind the illusion of personality. Without the Soul, the personality couldn't exist, for it is a child of the Soul; but at the same time the ego can create an artificial reality, as if in separation from the Soul. The evolution of intelligence is very mysterious. It is the child which makes the mother discover herself as mother. And it is because of the ego, the Soul can be awakened. In the illusion of personality, the true identity of the Soul is born. This reality works through the law of polarities. It is ignorance that gives rise to Enlightenment. The Soul, through the illusion of personality, the incomplete identity, finally discovers herself. It is a moment of celebration, for the deepest purpose of entering this dimension of suffering has been fulfilled.

The Soul is the knowing of one's own identity, which can be experienced on many levels, depending on the awakening. This knowing is based on feeling, which is directly intimate. The mind is the thinking and emotional extension of the Soul in the world. Prior to awakening, the Soul doesn't know its true identity, and therefore is identified with the mind and lost in the personality.

What is really the Soul? Yes, it is Me, the "I" that is directly recognized in the heart and that embraces all of our being. It is the unique taste of Me, the child of the Beloved. The experience of the Soul is one of bliss, fullness and warmth. To feel the Soul is to be touched by the Beloved. It is an experience of the celestial realm; the realm of purity, beauty, kindness and love. The inner stillness of our being seems like a "natural state," but it is not what I am. I am something much more subtle. The Soul is not the "I Am." The "I Am" is impersonal and universal. The Soul is absolutely personal. It dwells within the Heart, but awakens through the I Am. It is the Soul that everyone possess, but that is so rarely seen. This is amazing. Not to see the Absolute can be understood, for it is a secret dimension in some way; but not to see the Soul? Not to see our true identity? It seems like an irony. The Soul is not just the Heart. She is within the Heart. She is what is "Me" within the heart. It is so simple and so subtle at the same time.

Only when the Heart center is open, does one discover that the most intimate, personal and direct experience of oneself, takes place in the Heart. The Soul becomes awakened. This is what "I am"—the fullness and warmth within my own Heart. I am the Soul, the child of the Creator. That's what I am. When this is realized, the sage again becomes innocent, the Buddha becomes the child, and the most beautiful flower of evolution opens fully.

The Soul is, however, not simply the sense of "Me;" it is that in Me which meets the Divine. The Soul is eternally the child of the Beloved, of her divine Mother. The personality becomes adult, accumulates experiences and knowledge and is always the outcome of the past. What is becoming an adult? What is accumulating experiences throughout life, hiding more and more behind the thick wall of insensitivity called common sense? Issues of survival, mind games and sinking deeper and deeper in the falsity of the ego identity, closes our Heart and takes us away from innocence, sensitivity and beauty. The Heart is the only truth, our only identity and the essence of real life. All else is a form of death. We live in a society of robots; we live among humans who have lost their souls. That's why it is the plane of suffering. It is the world of suffering not because we have desires and attachments, but because our Souls are not awakened.

The Heart is the place where we meet the Divine and at the same time it is the Divine herself. The Heart is multidimensional, being placed in the human dimension and yet rooted in the source of Mystery. The Heart belongs to the Creator but expands into its individual expression. In this way, we are one with the Creator and separated from her at the same time. The Soul is that which knows the oneness and the separation. The experience of the oneness is possible only because one can feel the separation. That's why being a Soul is unique in Creation. There are many dimensions of existence and intelligence, but being completely one with the Divine or completely separated from her— both the joy of Oneness and the sorrow of separation are not experienced.

The foundation of the Heart is the Divine herself. The Heart of the human being is the Soul. But the depth of the Heart is the space of divinity between the Soul and the Beloved. Neither one nor two, but The Mystery.

The Journey to Our True Identity

The Soul is the secret behind the journey of individual evolution. Originally the Soul is unaware of herself; she gives rise to evolution while herself remaining in the shadow. In the beginning, the Soul is just a blueprint of future recognition, a blueprint that knows all the steps in-between. She seeks herself and her Creator, the Beloved. This journey is taking place through the evolution of consciousness, intelligence and sensitivity. The Soul cannot discover herself fully until those faculties are completely open. This journeying into true identity is an amazing adventure of the Soul. It is beyond words. Let us look at the different stages of this search that is happening in the arms of eternity.

In the human being, the Soul becomes self-conscious as an ego. The ego is her false identity. Ego has no reality apart from the movement of intelligence. The ego is a momentary act of consciousness evolving around the self-image. The ego always relates any act of recognition to an imaginary subject which common sense translates as "me" but devoid of any substantial identity. The ego is real as a function, but not as an identity. Who is thinking, who is feeling, who is behind the self-image? We cannot come to a conclusion too quickly; to make a mistake about this is much easier than to find the correct answer.

When the Soul sees that the identification with thoughts and feelings is not her real identity, she starts to seek within the consciousness for her true face. It is usually at this stage when one discovers the state of Presence. The Soul is experiencing her pure "I Am" for the first time. It is so easy to stop at this stage, assuming that this is our true identity. So many have stopped here, convinced that this is the end of the journey, but it is much too soon.

When the I Am is awakened, what actually is realized? We need to see that the only way the Soul can experience herself is through consciousness. Consciousness in the global sense means "to know." Without consciousness there is no knowing; it is a tool for knowing. The ego, for example, is a mental and psychological movement of consciousness, that is, of knowing. That's why when the ego is born, the Soul knows a part of herself, although not her true identity. The I Am is the essence of consciousness. The moment the Presence is born, the chaotic movement of consciousness is transcended in its center of stillness. When the Soul discovers the Presence, we can say she has found the tool through which she can recognize herself. Through the Presence, the Soul is conscious of herself as pure consciousness. It is like seeing the crystal clear mirror in which pure knowing can be reflected. Who is the one in front of that ancient mirror? Am I the Presence, or is there something more? Is the mirror only reflecting the mirror? The Soul has discovered the tool by which she can recognize herself, the essence of consciousness, but still it is not her true identity.

The Soul is looking for happiness and completion. When the Soul sees that being in the I Am cannot fulfill her, for this state doesn't have the qualities of complete rest and ease, she provokes the shift to the Absolute State. In the Absolute State, the Soul recognizes herself as that which was never born, the Unborn source of Consciousness. In the Absolute State, the Soul, thanks to consciousness, recognizes that which is prior to consciousness, prior to any experience. Here she has the experience of absolute rest and ease. She feels relieved from the movement of consciousness, abiding finally in the place of unconditional peace. At this moment the Soul might conclude: "I am That," "I am not Consciousness, I am the Unborn." But the journey is not completed yet.

Although the Absolute has been found and the peace realized, still the true identity of the Soul has not been recognized. Who is behind the sense of I Am? Who recognizes the Absolute State? Who feels this amazing rest of being in the Absolute? It is not simply "Consciousness" and it is not "nobody." There is something more to it, much more. This "more" is Me, my True identity. What is it? My true identity is not personality, not the I Am, not the Absolute State. The ego is just a movement of my intelligence; the I Am is the essence of that by which I am conscious and I can experience knowing; the Absolute is simply my foundation, the source of my beingness on which I eternally rest. But who or what am I?

All our life we experience Me as a feeling of "being oneself," mixed with our longings, desires, fears and moods. What is the center of identity behind my experience of life? What is the intimate core behind the sense of myself? The Soul, expanding into the different realms of consciousness and intelligence, is coming closer and closer to awakening herself to herself, as herself. This awakening can take place only if the maturity of intelligence meets the depth of sensitivity within the Heart. I am that which I feel directly in my Heart as myself. The utmost intimate touch of my own recognition of myself is absolutely personal. Humility, innocence and sensitivity meet in the Heart as a direct knowing of myself as myself.

Because the Soul recognizes herself in the realm of Consciousness, reaching the higher levels of awareness is very important. Only if the pond is still and silent, can the reflection of the moon be clear. The Soul can be experienced without the awakening of the I Am or the Absolute State, but in this case the experience is very vague and quickly disturbed by the restless mind.

In the background of the Soul's evolution, is her blueprint, the plan of her destiny, the ultimate vision of her fulfillment. It is the loving control of the Soul's path that comes from the Source itself. It is nothing else, but the force of Evolution. The destiny of the Soul is rooted in the wisdom of the Universe, in the ecological system of Oneness. The ultimate future of the Soul brings her past into the present and the present into the future. The unconscious Soul is being taken care of and led in many mysterious ways to its future fulfillment. The eternally awakened Heart of the Creator embraces within itself the Soul's destiny and her relative freedom, like the mother who brings the unconscious child into its future.

We are coming to the full understanding of what the I Am really means. This I Am is something much more than the state of Presence, the experience of Impersonal Consciousness. The I Am state, although it is based on the experience of Amness, at the same time refers to itself as "I." We might think that it is simply a creative faculty of our intelligence to relate to itself, but although it is correct, it doesn't bring us to the essence of that Me which I am. It is the Soul that is experiencing all states, knowing at the same time, in her own way, this very truth. The "I" is the Soul and the "Amness" is the Consciousness. Ultimately the I Am announcement refers to the oneness of the Soul, the Consciousness and the Absolute. I Am means that Me, the Soul, resting upon the Ultimate State is recognizing herself in the mirror of Consciousness.

The Consciousness without the Soul represents the quality of isness, the recognition of Being, the pure information of existence. In the case of human beings, this pure information is mixed with the sense of "I" which is at this point a reflection of the unconscious Soul. The sense of "I" in its fullness is a unity of the Presence and the Soul. When the Presence and the Soul are not awakened, the sense of "Me" refers to the illusion of the imaginary ego-image. The Soul is a combination of the Presence and the Heart, experienced in a unique and intimate way. Although it has universal qualities, it is at the same time absolutely personal. The sense of "I" ultimately belongs to the Soul and only to the Soul.

Let us repeat. In the beginning, the Soul experiences herself as personality and the mind. She is at this stage, completely unconscious. Later she discovers her Amness and transcends the mind. Afterwards, she slips to the Absolute and reaches Pure Rest. And finally she discovers her Heart, and in this Heart—herself.

There is both the Soul that experiences and the experience of the Soul. To experience the Soul is to know what one truly is. To find the Soul is to experience within the Heart the deepest, the most intimate, personal and unique feeling of Me. It is quite simple. But the Soul is covered by layers of insensitivity, ignorance, restless mind and false identifications. The Soul can realize herself fully only if she meets the Beloved. The Soul in reality exists only in relation to the Beloved. Like a ray of the Sun, although we can look at it separately, it exists only because of the Sun and through the Sun. The Soul is a reflection of the Beloved within the Heart.

The Beloved

One can realize the Emptiness and not to see the Sun within it. This Sun is the Creator, the Divine force of love and wisdom behind the power of Creation. The Beloved cannot be felt unless the Soul is awakened. To experience any state we need certain faculties. For example, to experience the Absolute, the consciousness must be completely mature and sensitive. Similarly one cannot sense the Creator unless the Soul has flowered. The Soul is the link between an individual being and its Creator; there is no other link. The Creator has no name and doesn't belong to any religion or cult created by ignorant people. She doesn't belong to any human tradition and can be known only in the realm of aloneness, where the Soul directly prays to the Beloved and is touched by her. There is no medium, no priest, no church in-between. There is only the Soul and the Beloved, nothing else.

We have left the dimension of Consciousness and the Absolute. Now we are entering the dimension of the Divine. One becomes a child again, but a child that carries within itself the sage, the Enlightened essence. When the suffering has been left behind and the inner peace realized, it is time to return to the positive, to beauty, ecstasy and prayer. The dimension of love, beauty and grace is all around us. The Beloved, the Creator, is living secretly in each one of us. This can be realized only when our heart and intelligence reach a deep level of maturity. The Beloved is. If we look at the deepest longings of our heart, none is deeper than the desire to be seen and touched by that which gave rise to our existence, by the Beloved. When Grace enters our life, all becomes transformed to the core. When the Divine touches us, there is no end to tears of joy and gratitude.

We all want to be loved, but we do not know where the love can come from. Behind this longing, there is the subtle knowing of our divine inheritance. The Soul knows that it is just a child of the Beloved, a child resting eternally in her arms of love and grace. All is well, for the Beloved Is. Only those open to Grace can see it. We have some freedom, strength and will but where can our will and freedom lead us ultimately? What else can we do but surrender to the higher love of the Creator? The child knows that it belongs to its mother—where else could it go? We are children of love; we come from the Divine Mother. It is our inheritance and our dignity. Surrendering to the Beloved is the highest the wisdom of the heart.

Is our heart open to hear the whisper from the Beyond? Do we feel that we are surrounded by love? These questions are not only beautiful, these are the questions indicating truth. Only the heart that is sincere, humble and tender can enter the realm of Divinity. Ultimately we all feel alone in this world, even among people, for in truth our being cannot be fulfilled unless we meet the Creator, the Beloved. It is the only water that can quench our thirst. Grace exists. Only those who experience it have no doubts. But there is a wisdom behind Grace. It comes when the timing is right and when the Soul is ready to receive it. The Beloved can quench all our longings, and it is only she that can do it. For all is happening by the power of the Creator. All is happening through the

Beloved. Even the realization of the Soul and higher states of consciousness take place only through the Grace of the Beloved. We have some relative freedom and our efforts certainly matter, but the transformation can occur only as an intervention from the Beyond. There is no other way in this dimension of suffering and slow evolution.

The mystery of the Soul is that although she dwells within the Heart of the Beloved, she is at the same time able to feel herself as separated from the Beloved. Because of this separation, the meeting and its joy can take place. The Soul is deeply sad, being separated from the Beloved. But she is also full of joy, bliss and love, for it feels the Beloved within and without. As the Sun is the secret of the shining moon, so is the Beloved the secret of the Soul. The Soul is simply a reflection of the Infinite, the spark of eternal fire which comes from the Heart of the Creator.

Desirelessness and the Soul-Desire

The pure purpose of the quest for desirelessness is to reach the dimension that is empty of personal self. On the relative level, this means that one gives up his/her identification with personal well being, so to speak. The personal self always must more or less face a lack of fulfillment in the realm of desire. This is the nature of our reality. For this reason, disidentification with the ego and identification with the empty Self bring a certain solution to this problem. But when we close the door against the thief, the beautiful guest cannot visit us either. Desirelessness is a solution to the problem of suffering, but when taken as absolute, it will block any possibility of expansion.

An important problem with the teachings of the past is that their simplistic conclusions do not reflect the richness of reality. Even though some masters, without a doubt, have realized the Soul, their intellect and the conceptual tools of their particular traditions are not able to distinguish the experience of the Soul from the experience of the Self, or to understand them in a universal context. The understanding and the experience always go hand in hand. Without the differentiation between the Soul and the Self we will never be able to grasp the paradox of <u>right</u> desire in the realm of desirelessness.

Expansion can occur only because of desire. But ego desires do not bring expansion, for the ego acts outside the field of universal Oneness. The desire which brings evolution always comes from the Soul. The Soul's desire is nothing but the way the Creator wills to expand through this particular individual expression. The desire of the Soul is present in the context of Oneness. The Soul has got to evolve. It cannot stop, for to stop is to negate life, to negate Creation. The concept of desirelessness negates life. It's aim is only to exit from life. The Soul, because she is directly linked with the Beloved is one with the purpose of evolution and is aiming only toward completion and positive fulfillment.

Behind the existence of every Soul is a divine plan that goes much further than what we call human evolution. The purpose of evolution is not to reach nirvana or dissolution, but to infinitely expand into the heart of the Mystery. Only this understanding brings real freedom. The negative conclusion of Buddhism ultimately brings an impasse, for it blocks the flow of evolution.

Nevertheless we must not forget that the Soul which is not resting upon the Absolute is incomplete and separated from the Source. We can be one with the Source and separated from the Creator, or we can be in direct connection with the Creator while separated from the Source. When these two aspects are integrated, the evolution of the Soul is in complete alignment with Universal Intelligence, and has support from above and below, from within and without. This is the law.

We experience various kinds of desires. From the material, physical, emotional and intellectual to the purely spiritual, such as reaching the state of Presence or discovering the Soul. Many are valid and important to be fulfilled. But how do we know if our desire is coming from the Soul or from the ego-subconscious? Is our desire arising from our past conditionings or is it a right response to the necessity of the Now? The only way we can know is by looking within our heart, becoming one with our Soul, and feeling deeply whether or not this particular desire is what we really want. If the heart feels nourished and deeply responds "yes" to what we desire, that is what we call the Soul's desire. As we mature in our spiritual journey and enter the inner realms of silence of being, awaken the heart and evolve in our creative intelligence, a clarity is born that translates itself as sensitivity. It senses and discerns what is coming from the personality and what is coming from our Soul. It knows our Soul's desires. To be in touch with our Soul's desires means to flow in harmony with the wide river of personal and universal evolution.

The Soul and the Absolute

In the Absolute State, the energy of the personality is constantly being pulled to its original absence. One becomes disidentified with reality as if one was without much will to live. The state itself, although with some positive qualities of complete unchanging peace and silence, is more neutral than positive. It represents the absence of suffering and freedom from consciousness. From the perspective of this state, all people are seen to be suffering. But how the state presents itself to the one in the state, is more like an absence of the negative than a presence of the positive. Because the "absence" is much stronger than the presence, one is "not really here." Because we see that the personality is not really our identity, while the Absolute is rather our non-identity, we have no center and we live "nowhere". It is freedom but not happiness. From the higher perspective, one sees that the Absolute State is not beyond suffering because our true identity has not been awakened yet. Our Soul is crying within our unawakened heart. It is possible for one in the Absolute State to even commit suicide, for living in emptiness is against our nature.

We must awaken the Soul to find our true identity. When the heart center is open, one meets at last the essence of oneself. From abiding in ignorance we shifted to the non-abiding of the original state, and there at last we woke up to abiding in our true identity. That which we are is something very personal, very gentle, sweet and fragrant. Meeting the Soul changes the quality of our whole being. The coolness of the Absolute becomes filled with warmth and sweetness. The deep rest, innocence and beauty create one whole. This is what bliss is: the Absolute meeting the Soul. Only this.

The opening of the heart changes also the quality of the recognition of the Absolute. The state becomes even more appreciated. It is only the Soul that can have the highest appreciation of the Ultimate Rest. On the other hand, it is in this Rest that the Soul can experience herself fully, because for the first time she has a foundation. The experience of the Soul, with its beauty and sensitivity occurs together with the experience of infinite Rest. The Rest gives depth to the Soul and the Soul gives sweetness to the Rest. In the moment of integration we cannot separate them, for they become one. It is here that the outer and the inner for the first time merge. One cannot say if one is inside or outside. One is nowhere, but this "nowhere" is the Heart of the Universe, the Beloved Herself.

The Suffering of the Soul

Why are we born as human beings? Why do we have a body? Why do we have to suffer so much? The experience of being human is very unique. It is only in the body that the Soul can be experienced, and it is only in the human body that the Soul can be awakened. This is the law.

There are many other beings in the universe that represents various stages of evolution, but they do not have a Soul. These beings and entities do not have a sense of "Me"—they do not experience separation. It is only in the body that separation can be experienced. Why must we experience separation? Isn't it an illusion? Isn't it something negative in itself? We are touching here something immensely profound—the mystery of being human.

The purpose of being in the body and experiencing separation is to realize the Soul. The Soul can be realized only through the experience of suffering. Suffering is possible only in the body, for it is only in the body that the Soul can feel separated from the Creator. The deepest purpose of suffering is to realize the Soul. It is only because we experience suffering that we can experience joy. It is only because we feel separated from the Beloved that we can experience Grace and Oneness. Other beings do not experience Oneness, for they are permanently one with the Beloved. They do not experience happiness, for their state is one of permanent joy and contentment. The human being is very special, for it lives in the realm of polarities.

The sense of Me can arise only if one is in a situation of separation from the Beloved. From the ultimate perspective, there is only one Me—the Beloved. To experience the sense of Me is a real miracle, a transcendental paradox. We must see that at the moment the Me arises, the separation from the Creator is present. For this reason the past traditions attempted to negate the Me, calling it illusion and ignorance. But to negate Me is itself an illusion. Me is real, for the separation from the Beloved is real and has a noble purpose. Unless the true meaning of the Me is discovered, we cannot know the purpose of being human.

We have got to see what the essence of separation is. The Soul is not the so called ego-image. Ego is a mental self-reference. The Soul knows herself directly. Of course, the element of intelligence is very important in the recognition of the Soul, but this intelligence has nothing to do with creating mental concepts. This intelligence serves the heart and rests in the heart.

Who is experiencing the sorrow of separation? Who is that one? The traditional inquiry brings us to the state of I Am or Presence. But this is incorrect. The Presence doesn't experience anything, for it is itself just an experience. That which experiences the sorrow of separation is Me. But the irony is that although everyone has a Me, few know what this Me in truth is. Only the awakening of the heart allows us to experience our Soul. The realized Soul is awakened to herself in the heart. She is not just the heart. Me and the heart meet. Realization of the Soul is not complete unless she clearly sees herself as separated from the Beloved. As the baby exists only because of its mother, so the Soul *is,* only because of the Beloved.

The full realization of the Soul points in two directions. One is the experience of the Soul in itself, the fullness of the heart merged with our unique sensitivity. The second is feeling the Beloved. Feeling the Beloved brings, at the same time, the experience of separation and oneness, joy and sadness. The Soul is in herself a combination of joy and sadness. The sadness we speak about is not from our past—it is an existential sadness. It is the sadness of the Soul being separated from the Beloved. It is only through this sadness that the Soul can be discovered, not otherwise. The sadness links the Soul with the Beloved, and through this link joy arises.

It is only because we are in the body that we have a Soul. Only because we suffer can we realize our Soul. The suffering *is not* the purpose, but suffering *has* a purpose. Awakening to the Soul and to the Beloved can occur only if one passes through the depth of suffering. To realize the Soul is to see the essence of separation. All suffering ultimately points to the subject. I am suffering... I am suffering(!)—why? Why am I here? Who am I? Who has brought me here? If these questions are asked within our heart–the prayer is born.

The prayer is a love affair of separation and oneness between the Creator and the Soul. In reality, it is the suffering that allows us to fully experience our separation. From this comes prayer and openness to the Beloved. When the Soul is touched by the Beloved she is deeply moved and full of gratitude. The true liberation is not to realize that we have "no self" but the opposite: to discover our Soul and her separation from the Creator. Only this can bring us back to the Beloved. It is like a child who has realized that she has gotten lost from her mother. She feels despair, suffering and loneliness. These are the basic experiences of the Soul.

But when the mother is found, the child is immediately fulfilled and full of joy. The Grace of the Creator is all around us. But there is no higher Grace than that which brings us to the realization of the Soul. And it cannot happen without suffering. That's why the Grace of the Beloved allows us to suffer. But the closer we are to our true identity, the less we suffer. Bliss, joy and fulfillment replace our pain. At this point we see the wisdom of evolution and the presence of the divine law behind it. To be born is painful. So it is painful to give birth to the Soul. It happens amid tears, but those tears wash our heart before the divine communion with the Beloved. And those same tears are eventually transformed into tears of joy and gratitude. This is the Divine Alchemy...

The Soul and the Beloved: Unity and Separation

If the Soul was only one with the Beloved, the Soul would cease to exist. The Soul is the Beloved, but the Beloved that sees herself as a Soul. In this seeing, the Beloved is separated from herself. This is the mystery of Creation. These are not only beautiful words, but a reflection of the Truth.

How can we experience the Beloved? How can we see and feel the Beloved? It is extremely difficult to grasp the Beloved for the simple reason that she is not separated from us. The Soul is separated from the Creator but the Creator is not separated from the Soul. Without the opening of the Heart, we cannot even dream about touching upon the dimension of the Divine. The Heart is the entrance. The Soul herself rests deeply in the Heart. The Heart resting within itself is the Soul; not the Heart that moves outward, but the Heart that sees itself, feels itself and surrenders to itself.

The Soul in her natural state, is the Soul at rest. She rests in herself fully self-contained. When thoughts or feelings enter, the Soul experiences herself in motion. Rest and motion are the two fundamental characteristics of the Soul. They are interwoven together, interchanging and complementing each other.

In the search for our true identity, we must find our Soul and the place in which she abides. The "amness" of the Soul, the energy of her consciousness rests in the

Absolute, but where does the Soul herself dwell? When the Soul awakens to herself within the Heart, she becomes one with herself. But when we explore deeper the ultimate frontiers of our identity, a new understanding becomes revealed. We discover that the Soul in reality can rest only in the Beloved herself. The Soul can not rest in herself exclusively for she doesn't exist apart from the Creator. The Soul exists only in the Beloved. When the Soul rests in herself, she truly rests in the Heart of the Creation.

What we call the "Soul in rest" is the state of oneness with the Beloved. It is the Beloved herself. In any moment, the Soul can wake up to herself and the feeling of Me, which gives rise to the Separation. It is only because of this state that we can pray, have gratitude and experience our Soul. The prayer is not directed outwardly, neither is it directed inwardly. The prayer starts in the Heart where the feeling of separation is born, and reaches the same Heart that is the Beloved herself. The prayer is born in separation and dissolves in Oneness. The separation of the Soul and the Beloved, and their oneness, are One.

Without finding the Soul we cannot know that we are one with the Creator. To be one means—to be one. It is not just a poetic or philosophical concept. The doorway to the experience of this oneness is our true identity, the Soul. It is only the Soul that is one with the Beloved, not the ego. To be what we truly are, is to be one with the Beloved. We do not need to "become" one with her—this oneness is already present.

Where is the Beloved? How can the Beloved be found? How can the Soul know the Beloved? These questions are truly beautiful. This inquiry leads us not to the satisfaction of the mind, but to ecstasy. The pure understanding that is born in the Heart gives rise to the highest ecstasy, to the ecstasy of the Divine. It is not only the ecstasy of the Soul discovering the Beloved—it is the ecstasy of the Beloved discovering herself.

When the Soul is awakened, she knows herself in a most intimate way. Nevertheless she may still be unable to recognize the Beloved. We can say that in this case, the Soul has not been fully realized. To realize the Soul fully, feeling her is not enough; a subtle understanding, a deep knowing within the actual experience of the Soul is absolutely necessary. To realize the Soul means to enter the realm of the Beloved. But similar to the realization of the Absolute, one can enter the realm of the Beloved and not recognize it. And only this recognition brings the full understanding, completion and ecstasy. This recognition reveals finally and doubtlessly that which we truly are: (The) Divine.

How can the Beloved be recognized? The Beloved is the secret of the Absolute State—its inner treasure. The Beloved can be felt, as long as the Heart is experienced, but it can be directly touched only in the Absolute State. Why? Because she is the secret of the Absolute and can be recognized fully only in complete rest, in the original state. The Soul always experiences the dynamic quality of feeling herself within the heart space as the most intimate touch of Me. Where is this touch of Me arising from? The closer we come to our true identity, the more we see that the Soul at complete rest ceases to be a Soul, for it loses the quality of being separated. The Soul at complete rest is the Beloved herself. This is the highest revelation about our true identity.

The Beloved cannot be grasped, but can be clearly experienced. The Soul is that which meets the Divine. In this meeting, the Soul is dissolved into her deeper identity. But though she becomes dissolved, in some mysterious way, the Soul continues to exist, and recognizes That in which she is being dissolved. This is the miracle of the meeting with the Beloved. Because the Soul is present, the Beloved can be met; and only because the Soul can be dissolved, is the Beloved met. The Soul, therefore is the Beloved. The Beloved, therefore is the Soul...

Will and Grace

It is the law that <u>only if</u> a human being has done enough effort on his/her part, can Grace enter from the beyond. It always enters at the right time. The Soul receives help in her journey, but she must reach maturity on her own. In truth, any major shifts and transformations in our life are caused by intervention from the Beyond.

Human beings are quite helpless creatures. The most a person can do is to bring oneself to the verge of a possible expansion. From that place Grace enters. The effort, inquiry and suffering allow maturity and sensitivity to grow. Intelligence and consciousness must evolve. The heart needs to become more and more pure and sensitive. Our sincerity, striving and prayer invite the Grace of the Beloved into our life. Without Grace we would be unable to come close to the Divinity.

The true definition of a human being is: the child of the Beloved. We did not bring ourselves here. Ultimately, we did not even create our karma. Without the Beloved we are utterly helpless, lost and miserable. The importance of Grace doesn't take from us our dignity and nobility. The opposite is true. We are noble only because of the Beloved. The Beloved is All That Is. The existence of Grace links us with our true identity. Only being touched by Grace allows us to open in gratitude to the Beloved.

We are only the children of our divine Mother. Her love, kindness and wisdom are all that we have. On our own, we are like empty shells. Nothing is there. It is our Divine inheritance that gives us worth and dignity. It is all about knowing who we truly are. Unless we wake up to the reality, we live in an illusory world. And no nobility or dignity are found in illusion.

Enlightenment to the Heart

As there exists an Enlightenment to the Presence and Enlightenment to the Absolute, so there exists an Enlightenment to the Heart. It has nothing to do with cultivating certain qualities like compassion or loving kindness. These are ultimately just the expressions of an awakened Heart. The Heart is a dimension of its own, which links us with our Soul and with the Beloved. Without an awakened Heart, one cannot be complete. The Heart is absolutely important, for it is only through the Heart that we can experience richness, beauty and love. The Heart is a gateway to the Divine, a secret passage.

The Heart can be awakened before or after reaching the higher levels of consciousness. However, the Heart can be experienced in its depth only from the state of the Absolute. On the other hand, one can be in the Absolute State with a completely closed Heart. In the middle of our chest there is the secret cave of our Soul. Although we feel it in our physical body, it is rooted in the dimension of the Beyond, the Celestial Realm.

The Heart is the source of perception-feeling, the source of sensitivity. Because we are hurt in our childhood and later, we build many layers of protection around our Heart to avoid pain. So our contact with the Heart space becomes weaker and weaker until it becomes completely frozen. Most people live with what we could call: the minimum Soul. This minimum Soul allows us to experience some feelings of kindness and good intention, without which we would become completely neurotic. The minimum of heart prevents us from become inhuman, but is not enough to truly live. The frozen heart is an essential problem of human evolution. It is a big challenge to open our heart while living in a world which is insensitive and immersed in ignorance and darkness. But without an awakened Heart, we might as well be dead. We need to allow ourselves to again be innocent and vulnerable. This is the price we pay for our Soul. It is a bargain for the Soul is priceless. In reality we have nothing to defend but our illusions and misery.

How can we open the Heart? How can we melt the frozen shield around our Heart and access the warmth within it? Usually it takes some time. We need a clear intention that we want to regain our heart. Putting our hands on our chest, feeling our Heart, praying to the Beloved, listening to music that touches and moves us are ways of getting in touch with our Heart. Energy healing is very important, as well as being in the loving environment. Most helpful is to have an intimate connection with someone with an awakened Heart. As in the case of Enlightenment to the Absolute, the dimension of the Heart can be transmitted directly. Ultimately the full Enlightenment to the Heart occurs only through Grace. We should never forget that there are beings, energies and archetypes in this Creation, who always respond to our expansion, and doubtlessly answer our longings and prayers. Grace is not something unusual—we are surrounded by Grace.

Prayer is extremely important, for it is only the One who created our Heart that can open it. No healing is possible without the Creator. Buddhism speaks about the law of karma, but who created karma? In reality, we are responsible for our lives only to a very small extent.

It is only the One who brought us here that can lift us up to Divinity. In prayer, we feel our Heart and the One who created it. We feel our separation from our Divine Mother and our deep connection with her. Prayer is not a formula or an empty ritual. It is the utmost direct and intimate connection with our Creator.

When we feel this connection in the depth of our Heart, and at the same time feel our suffering, loneliness, isolation and deep sadness, we ask for healing and help. We express fully what we are longing for, knowing that without this force that gave rise to the Creation, we are utterly helpless. Prayer, real prayer, opens the door to the Beyond. The Beloved sees only our Heart. She doesn't see our mind, for it is empty of divine substance. She sees the Heart, for she is the Heart. The moment we acknowledge fully our pain, we are for the first time, in touch with our Soul. That which touches us deeply is always our Soul. Only in this space, can we ask for healing and help. Only here, are we truly seen. To be seen by the Beloved is the highest Grace. Nothing is higher than this, indeed it is the purpose of our life: to realize our separation from the Creator and to be seen by her. This is the most moving experience of all.

When in due time, the Heart is healed and the energy of the Divine can flow through, the totality of our being becomes centralized in the Heart space. This is what is called: Enlightenment to the Heart. The ice surrounding our chest melts, and what remains is the sweetness of the Heart, the warmth within, the touch of the Divine, the kiss of the Beloved. The one who is seen, who is touched, finally enters the realm of the Divine, the Celestial Realm.

Buddha Mind and Christ Consciousness

In these days of our Spiritual evolution as seekers, it is a common belief to assume that the notions "Buddha Mind" and "Christ Consciousness" represent the same Enlightened state of human spirit that reaches the ultimate. This popular and rather simplistic conclusion does not reflect reality. It is extremely important to understand that the revelation of sages who reached the Inner State and the one of saints who have realized the Divine are not the same. They represent, in fact, two different aspects of human illumination. Our concern is not to evaluate which one has the higher importance but to see really what the complete self-realized human being is. It is about us—about our wholeness. That to which we refer as the Buddha Mind and Christ Consciousness, on the deeper level, are the archetypes of our inner reality. So to know them fully is to know oneself.

The insight of Buddha pointed to the realization of the Source of all existence. He found that the essence of our being, prior to manifestation of individual personality, is one with the source of creation. This is what he called liberation. In the moment of his great Enlightenment, he recognized clearly that at the roots of our individual existence there is an absolute presence of the eternal Self, which in itself represents the unity of emptiness, silence and peace. He becomes the master of "Pure Being." This condition refers to the experience in which the individual consciousness becomes one with the silence and absolute rest of the primordial timeless state. When the illusion of a limited personal self was seen through—the universal oneness and peace were revealed. This is the realization of the unborn, silent or empty realm of existence.

The core of Christ's message is the Heart, which is the seat of the Soul. The experience of the Soul links us with the Divine. The Self represents the transcendental impersonal aspect of our being, and the Soul, which is the essence of sensitivity, represents the unique expression of the Creator as an individual Heart. Buddha discovered that liberation frees us from individuality. Christ discovered that one is always a child of the Divine, a child of the Creator, and that which links us eternally with the Beloved, is our own Heart. These two seemingly contradictory conclusions reflect the whole of Reality. They complement each other, touching different spheres of our being. We need to see that the Self and the Soul, though belonging to different dimensions of existence, together constitute our wholeness.

From the point of view of the spiritually integrated person, the Buddha Mind is experienced as the unconditioned stillness, clarity and peace of thoughtless awareness—which is the primordial womb of creation, while the Christ Consciousness is experienced as the fullness of Heart, the divine flavor of Heart, being embraced by the Beloved. When these two are integrated, one experiences a beautiful paradox of being simultaneously separated, that is, relating as a child to the Creator, and in the state of complete oneness with the Universe.

Beyond the mind, there is an absolute silence and

motionlessness of consciousness. This is the goal of every true meditator. We call it the Self. This is a state of total peace and disidentification with the personality. Although a high achievement, we are still not complete, because the Soul is missing. Resting in the absolute stillness of the original state, one is finally at peace but not yet fulfilled; one is at last free but still separated from the Beloved, from the highest ecstasy. To be fulfilled, freedom is not enough—the highest positivity has yet to be discovered, the divine Heart of the universe, the divine Mother, who rests always within our own Heart. The "Soul," is just a name for what we feel when touching our Heart. When the Heart is touched, it is always the Beloved, the Creator, who touches it. This is what prayer truly is—opening the heart to the Beloved and being touched by her.

The two magnificent human beings, Buddha and Christ, gave us amazing gifts. Both, with their authority, confirmed that there is, without shadow of a doubt, a direct connection with the source and the power of Creation. Buddha showed us that we can directly experience and become one with the timeless stillness of the primordial Self—that which is prior to Creation. He pointed to the dimension of the Self, the Godhead, the bottomless stillness of Being, the timeless Emptiness, which embraces the Soul and the Creator. Christ revealed to us that the love and grace of the Creator can be experienced directly within our own heart—for the Beloved and her child are one. His was the message of love and prayer, of direct connection with God, the Beloved. The original Self is like a pure, empty sky; the Creator, the Beloved is like the sun filling the emptiness with light and warmth. They cannot be separated, although we might realize them separately. To see the Creator without the Source is like seeing the sun without seeing the sky. To see the Source without the Beloved is like seeing the sky in the deep bottomless night. Both are incomplete.

The Soul without the Self has no roots, has no foundation in the inner realm. The Self without the Soul is only neutral, lacking love, lacking joy. It is like a flower without color and fragrance. The Source and the Beloved are the two fundamental aspects of Creation. Only after awakening to both within ourselves, can we experience wholeness. We are directly linked to the Divine, but the conscious illumination to this fact is a challenge of our evolution. This experience and understanding are not given—they must be awakened. When the Buddha Mind and the Christ Consciousness become one indivisible whole in each of us, the evolution of humankind can be said to have reached its highest and most noble destiny.

It is not enough to have a spiritual or mystical experience—the wisdom has to support it. Without wisdom and sensitivity there is no power of transformation, for one is not in alignment with the Truth. And it is only the Truth which can transform the ignorance into light. Now we understand clearly that in the world of real mystics there are only two possible experiences: that of the Soul and that of the Self; and they are not the same. More common is, of course, the experience of the Soul, for it dwells in the Heart of each one of us. To reach the Self, to reach the Buddha Mind, the unconscious and mechanical mind must be transcended. This is not an easy task, therefore only a few complete it fully. But if the mind is not transcended and inner silence is not reached, even the Soul can not be grasped fully. It is only the inner thoughtless silence that can give it roots–containing it within itself. The Self not only adds a new dimension to the Soul, but allows it to open fully, and to have finally a place of absolute rest. It is like seeing the moon in the lake—only when the water is calm and still, is the reflection clear and constant. Without the presence of pure thoughtless consciousness, the experience of the Soul cannot be contained for long, because the restless mind will soon stir the inner water.

The meeting of Buddha Mind and the Christ Consciousness gives rise to something totally new, which is the completion of the spiritual journey. As the Source of Existence is one with the mysterious force of Creation; as the Emptiness is one with the wisdom and love of the Beloved—so is our inner sun, the Soul, one with the absolute calmness of the inner sky, the Self. It is truly the Soul who wants to become one with the Self, and it is the Self who must discover the Soul, in order to complete itself. The journey to completion is a mystery, until it dissolves into its own goal.

IV

Realm of the Wholeness

IV

Realm of the Wholeness

Rest Within and Know That—I Am

The I AM is the center of the infinite Universe. The I AM is the Creator and her Creation. There is only one I AM: the Beloved. There is only one I AM, so know that I AM.

The Creation is an expression of the I AM, its extension. The recognition of the Creation without knowing the Creator is ignorance. And the awakening to the Creator without the total apperception of the Creation is incomplete. To experience the Beloved, the Soul drops to the depth of the Heart within. But although the depth of the I AM is recognized, its totality is not seen. It is only when the Inner is transcended that the seeing of All takes place.

The Absolute is that which allows the Creation to take place. The possibility of "not being" exists only due to the presence of the Absolute. That which is manifested can dissolve only in the Absolute. The quality of absence of the Absolute exists only from the perspective of that which is created, not from the Creator's. The Creator is always the I AM, and the Absolute is simply its foundation, without the polarity of being and not being. If there was only the Beloved, we would be unable to experience the state of deep sleep or death. The Beloved is eternally the I AM, but her Creation which is an expression of I AM, can cease to "be," due to the "absence" of the Absolute. The experience of the Absolute exists only for that which is created. There are two fundamental experiences of the Absolute. One is the full absence, that is, lack of consciousness and the second is the Absolute State. The "nothing" exists. That which receives presence into the absence is the nothing. The linear mind cannot comprehend that the nothing *is*; it is a dimension of pure isness. The absence is present—it is the foundation of the presence, which is present. For the Beloved, the Absolute is not experienced, because she is beyond the polarities of presence and absence.

The Me is an angle of perception through which the I AM is experienced. Me is an expression of the I AM, an expression that refers to itself as "I am" but which is not the I AM. In this referral, Me may think that it is the I AM itself, for Me discovers it as its own center of identity. If Me was the I AM, it wouldn't vanish in the deep sleep state. The Me is not the I AM, therefore I am not the I AM. <u>I am the perception of the I AM</u>. I am that which discovers the I AM, I am the taste of the unique perception of the I AM.

The origin of the Soul is the primal, unique taste of the I AM in its particular individual manifestation. The final vision, the blueprint of the Soul is the complete recognition of the depth of the I AM. There are many layers of perception of I AM, from the ego sense of I am, to the state of Presence, to the experience of deep rest in the Absolute, and finally to the rest in the Heart. That which is experienced in the depth of the Heart as I AM, is not Me, but the universal I AM or God. I am not the I AM. I am the unique way the universal I AM recognizes itself in Creation. I am not the I AM, but the experience of I AM.

When the inner is completed and transcended, the new perception arises which is born from the explosion into the totality of I AM. The Total Perception is directed neither within nor without, but sees into the realm between them. This "between" place is the dimension where the Creator and the Creation are met. The Total Perception is directionless and rests in the inner and outer simultaneously. It is not the so-called "suchness." The perception of suchness comes from the place of Inner. Suchness is the seeing of the Oneness, while the apperception we speak about is the Oneness itself.

The Total Perception occurs through the channel of Me, that is the particular and unique flavor of how the I AM perceives itself in Creation. That apperception is directionless, but contains within itself the Rest in the Absolute and the full and sudden awakening to the Now, which is the explosion of the I AM into I AM. The heart is the doorway, but when the inner is transcended the heart is no longer placed within. The realm of the Creator can be perceived only in the act of Creation. Perception is co-creation; The Total Perception, which is the Complete Understanding—is the Creation. Me, at the peak of its evolution, becomes one with the Creation. The Creation is occurring neither in nor out. It is an explosion of the I AM into I AM. It is the Now. Seeing this, rest within and know that I AM. Only I AM.

Samadhi: The Absence of Me?

There are many misunderstandings about the real meaning of the term "Samadhi." Particularly those conditioned by Hindu spirituality associate it with a trance-like absorption. To be totally "gone" is the highest spiritual attainment for them. The ability to fall into coma, using certain practices, elevate anyone to the rank of "holy one" or "sage" in the eyes of certain people with limited understanding. But the reality of Samadhi is much more complex than simple identification with trance or loss of consciousness. Because Samadhi refers to the state of absorption, we shall look upon two fundamental aspects that relate to the phenomena of absorption: one is the state of absorption itself, and the other, the simultaneous position of <u>Me</u>.

There are two essential realms of absorption, where the absorption takes place—the I Am itself, and the Absolute. Samadhi in the I Am is not complete, for it is not able to reach the state of complete Rest and Nondoing. The absorption takes place within the aspect of Being. The more the energy of Being is freed from the personal will, the deeper it is pulled by the gravitational force of the Absolute. But it is only when the gate to the Absolute opens, that the Being aspect of I Am reaches the Beyond and is entirely freed from the personal will.

Samadhi is not about the disappearance of Me. In the actual state of coma, Me is absent, but we certainly wouldn't call it Samadhi. It is only due to the presence of the Me that Samadhi can be experienced. Even in a trance-like Samadhi, a subtle element of Me is present. For Samadhi is <u>an experience</u> and not merely a state of being unconscious.

True Samadhi does not concern the absorption of Me. Me can be fully functioning while the <u>energy of being</u> is at complete rest, dropped into the original absence. Samadhi applies to the Being aspect of I Am, not to the whole of Me. The conscious presence of Me or its absorption, which is relative absence, is not directly connected with the unconditional Samadhi. In relative Samadhi, there is a movement of consciousness that goes in, deeper and deeper. This consciousness cannot go beyond itself. It is only when the Absolute is realized that consciousness drops to the Beyond. This aspect of consciousness that rests within the Absolute, transcends the polarity of going in or emerging out. The Absolute Rest allows the consciousness to be fully present, and allows Me to participate in the world and in its own evolution.

Only when we can fully see the elements which the I Am is composed of, do we have, for the first time, the ability to grasp the reality of Samadhi. Because Samadhi applies to the Being aspect of I Am, the presence of Awareness, the Heart and the Intelligence have no impact on the depth of absorption. Pure Rest is beyond the field of consciousness, although it is being experienced within the I Am. The presence of the Unborn and the flowering of evolution, that is, the I Am, become One.

Me in "Non-duality"

The essence of the "Non-dual" perception is the desire of a particular Me to identify itself with the Source and the Totality of Creation. In awakening to the Oneness, which is Enlightenment, Me may wish to negate its very own existence. Me wants deeply to dissolve its identity within the ocean of Existence. The personal wants to become the Impersonal, the Universal.

So the question arises: can Me really negate its own existence? Can it simply disappear in the experience of Wholeness? At this point one can see that Truth and Reality are subject to the interpretation of the individual Me with its unique psychology and desire to position itself in a way that suits its intelligence best. But one thing is clearly certain: for any proclamation of "I am That" to take place, the individual Me has got to be there to proclaim it. How could the Universal be expressed, without the existence of the particular? Me is the experiencer of all states and cannot cease to be present. When Me dissolves, one returns to the Original State, prior to consciousness.

Me is that which allows us to experience the I AM. The I AM which one experiences is not Me—it is that which created Me. One can never become the Creator. It is true that Self-realization is a state of complete Oneness with the universal I AM, but Me which experiences this Oneness *is not* this I AM. Me can disidentify with the whole universe, but is not able to identify with its Creator. The Self-realized Me rests upon the Ultimate Subjectivity and experiences it through <u>itself</u>. Me cannot become the Ultimate, no matter how deeply it is awakened to the dimension of Pure Rest and Wholeness. Why? For the very simple reason that Me always, regardless of the State it is in, <u>feels itself</u>.

The "philosophy" of Non-duality traditionally was designed to negate the essential presence of Me in all states and levels of experience. The nature of Me, is from a certain perspective, much more subtle than all the inner states, for it is the Nearest. Me cannot simply disappear in any state, for without Me the experience of that very state vanishes. What "I am" is not eternal though it evolves eternally within the universal I AM. It is born and it dies. It dies, and is reborn into a new Me. Me expands infinitely into the vastness of the Universal Intelligence. It is the journey of the Spirit into the ultimate experience of love, beauty and happiness.

It is possible to call the Creation an illusion, the Creator–emptiness, and the Soul–non-existent. This would be the shortest way to the impersonal. Seemingly, the impersonal is reached by the impersonal and dissolves into the impersonal. This is the ideal of Non-duality. But in truth, to meet the impersonal face to face, the personal must be there to face it. Here, the ultimate duality serves its supreme purpose, and Me rests in full acceptance of its supreme "dual" existence and truth.

Non-duality, without the awakening to Me, represents the Wholeness of Perception in which Me refuses to see itself as a dynamic and alive center of identity behind the Perceived. When Me is awakened to itself for the first time, the new and true Non-dual vision of reality is apperceived. In this apperception, the Wholeness embraces its very experiencer, the unique Soul, the intimate heart of Me, as itself. This Me is an indivisible part of the Ultimate Seeing. The Non-dual Perception is not the end of Seeing. The evolution into the Seeing of Reality does not have an end. And this evolution can take place only through the Me, the mysterious perceiver of the Universal I AM. This Perceiver is not separated from the Wholeness. It is this part of the Totality through which the Now becomes the Seen.

Intelligence: The Power of Recognition

Me is nothing but a flow of intelligence, which doesn't necessarily mean that Me is always "intelligent". Me is an evolution of intelligence into Reality. When Reality is met fully, the intelligence becomes transformed into pure knowing, which is complete into itself.

The role of intelligence in the recognition of inner states and outer reality is tremendously important. The traditional teachings do not acknowledge the correlation between the experience of the inner and that which is recognizing it. It is not only that our intelligence recognizes the inner states, but that this very intelligence is an inseparable part of those states. Even that which we call "Pure being" is nothing but a form of intelligence integrated energetically with the motionlessness of the original state. But without the faculty that allows us to know that we know, the experience of the inner is entirely meaningless. Our intelligence is truly multidimensional, for it touches many angles of knowing simultaneously. It is splendid and magnificent. This intelligence is capable of referring to itself in many ways. It can grasp the most subtle aspects of reality in the form of understanding. It is not enough to be awakened to the inner. One must also be awakened to the fact of being awakened to the inner.

We can say that there are two major levels of recognition of the inner states. First is the primal knowing, which is the energetic presence of the state itself. For example, the state of Presence introduces constant information of its existence into the subtle part of our consciousness, whether we are aware of it or not. The state recognizes itself as its own presence in a neutral way. The second level of recognition occurs when the intelligence of Me brings into a higher perspective the presence of what already is. It is only this intelligence that can give any value to the presence of <u>any</u> state. How the presence of the inner state is understood and appreciated depends exclusively on the level of evolution of the recognizing intelligence.

The depth of being, the clarity of the mind and the profound sensitivity of the heart create the complete field of intelligence. This intelligence, expressed through the channel of the individual in the process of growth, transcends more and more the frontiers of individuality, becoming transparent and melting with the wholeness of I AM. This intelligence, operating within the field of limitations, at the peak of its evolution, dissolves into the perfection of the all-embracing I AM. But although it has become transparent and melted with the knowingness of the Wholeness, it is capable of knowing it and referring back to itself. This is how the I AM is adventuring within the infinity of Being Itself.

The Final Revelation About Me

Me is the core-essence of being human. The actuality of Me is truly mysterious, for it is not a state. Because of its dynamic quality, Me cannot be pinpointed or grasped by the mind. Similar to the rainbow as an expression of white light, Me is real and mysteriously transparent at the same time. Me, like the rainbow, is a manifestation of the universal I AM. The Me is not the I AM—it is its child.

Within the borders of the all-embracing Universal Consciousness and the infinity of Universal Intelligence, the space of "not-knowing" is created, which is the essence of Me. To be born is to emerge into the not-knowing. The not-knowing is the space within which the conscious evolution of intelligence can take place. Evolution is an expansion of the relative within the Absolute, of the imperfection within the Perfection. When the relative, the limited perspective, is transcended in the apperception of Wholeness, the evolution stops and Me ceases to exist. The human Me can exist only in the realm of polarities, where not-knowing and knowing are interwoven. In spiritual evolution, Me transcends more and more the not-knowing, coming into the knowing. When the limits of expansion are reached, the human Me dissolves into the Beyond, which is Pure Knowing.

Me is not merely a state of ignorance, as some teachings proclaim. It is absolutely valid, for it allows the dynamism of evolution to take place. Ignorance exists within the Me but is not identical with it. Not-knowing is not the same as ignorance. Ignorance is simply a form of unconsciousness, while not-knowing means being faced with the unknown. It is a human situation and can take place only in the context of separation. In this dimension of Creation, Me is the link between Creator and the Universe. Me is the part of the Creator, of the I AM, that forms (in this particular angle of perception) the bridge with the wholeness of her Creation.

What is Me in itself? It is the field of separate identity, containing many qualities and functions such as having a physical form, thoughts, feelings, memory and a specific subconscious mind, linked with particular past experiences. But the essential feature of Me which allows one to experience all of these qualities as a part of "what I am" is the unique feeling and translation of the universal I AM, as my particular self—myself. Me is <u>a version</u> of the universal I AM that feels its unique flavor, in contrast to what is relatively within and relatively without. To give rise to the experience of polarities, the universal I AM creates within itself a relative perspective of separation; a version of itself, within which the Wholeness can, in an inexplicable way, "relate" to that very Wholeness.

The difficulty with grasping the nature of Me is that although it is an expression of Wholeness, it is separated from it at the same time. Like a crystal ball in a crystal ball, or a glass of water in the ocean, one and separated, separated and one. Me is not a state but a self-conscious movement of time. It cannot be grasped, but can be seen as it is. Spiritual evolution leads us not only beyond our individuality into the experience of the Wholeness, but into the final awakening to the Me itself. Me is that which allows us to experience the

Wholeness. In this experience, Me is transcended, but not annihilated—it remains an indivisible part of the apperception of that Wholeness.

Without the experience of Wholeness, Me in reality cannot be seen in its fullness. The Wholeness of I AM reflects back to the wholeness of Me. The Wholeness is I AM; The wholeness of Me is what "I Am," resting within the Totality. I am not the I AM, but the I AM is Me. What does it mean to experience the wholeness of Me within the Wholeness of I AM? It is to embrace all aspects of my unique self-conscious sensitivity and intelligence within the complete apperception of the I AM. What does it mean to experience the Wholeness of I AM through the wholeness of Me? Beyond the inner and the outer, the I AM is known directly as I AM. In this pure knowing, Me dissolves. But although it has dissolved, it experiences ultimate beauty, the ultimate ecstasy—it is being touched by the hand of the Divine Mystery.

Enlightenment to Me

Me is simply who one is. Unless the stable awareness and the quality of being is awakened, we are not able to experience Me. There must be continuity of experience, free from the mind, in order to become fully conscious of oneself. We can say that prior to Enlightenment, Me is not yet born. What exists is only a fragment of it, nothing more. Me is first an experiencer of ignorance and unconsciousness, the one who suffers and seeks freedom from it. After Enlightenment, Me is that which experiences peace, silence and stillness of the inner state. In both cases, Me refers to the <u>experienced</u>, to its "environment" so to speak. In both cases, Me is not aware of itself. Even if one becomes a Buddha and recognizes the Unborn, it is possible that Me still is not aware of itself.

The Final Enlightenment takes us beyond states: beyond the state of ignorance and the inner states as well. For the first time, Me discovers itself. It is neither in nor out. It is in a mysterious middle point where these realities meet. It can choose to rest in the inner or to participate in the outer. But when the Heart is awakened, Me experiences the fullness of itself in its own dimension. Realizing the inner states is not all that's required to enter the Divine. The Soul must be completely awakened to herself. Then, in the wholeness of herself, she reaches the ultimate expansion. Me does not dissolve but its frontiers merge within the Wholeness.

When Me directly refers to itself, that is, becomes

166 Enlightenment Beyond Traditions

attentive to itself, it has a crystallized and centralized quality. When it rests in itself, its knowingness, its experience of itself dissolves within the space of being. But prior to arriving at the Absolute State, the presence of Me, even in the state of rest, cannot free itself fully from the characteristic of being self-oriented; of referring to itself in terms of attention, recognition and energy. The Absolute State brings the quality of Pure Rest which allows the transcendence of will which is the indivisible part of the self-referral mechanism.

To rest in the Absolute is not sufficient however, in order to be free from the self-referral tendency. As we already know, although the will is transcended in the Absolute State, it is still present on the side of the Me. It is not how Me rests upon the Absolute, but how it rests upon itself that concerns us. How can Me transcend the will in the very experience of itself? How can the Me go beyond crystallization and its inherent mechanism of self-referral? It is only after reaching the continuity of the Presence, the Rest in the Absolute and the fullness of itself in the Heart, that the Me can rest, beyond any form of crystallization, in complete transparency dissolved into the Universal I AM. It is only when all states are transcended and the fullness of Me embraced within itself, beyond the inner and the outer, in the state of pure non-abiding, that one finally drops into ultimate transparency, the only true happiness.

The State of Ignorance

The state of ignorance refers simply to the level of evolution of consciousness that does not recognize the I Am. Consciousness is veiled by unconsciousness, being unaware of its own subjectivity. The state of ignorance is very difficult to describe, for it is not a state, but chaos. The subject is not present yet. It is only sensed in the trance of experiencing. The state of ignorance is very much like a dream.

The sense of Me is what makes us human. Everyone has this sense, and in reality it is the essence of being conscious. Because the human consciousness is exteriorized in the objective reality, unless it evolves, it is not capable of grasping the very subject of all experiences. The thing called "ego" is nothing but the sense of Me referring to objective reality. The ego-image is the way Me sees itself in relation to the world. There is nothing wrong with the ego or self-image. The ability to create a self-image allows us to survive in the world, as well as to evolve in all areas of reality. Our interest is not to eradicate the ego, but to see clearly what this Me is behind the ego's mechanism.

We can say that there are two dimensions of Me: one in motion, and one "in itself," so to speak. Me in motion, is the movement of intelligence, thoughts, feelings, the ability to create self-image and so forth. Me "in itself" is a complete and self-contained experience of our whole being, in the state of pure rest. Me "in itself" is what most people ignore, that is, are unaware of its very existence. Ignorance, in the case of human beings is very particular. All human beings sense the Me. That itself is a sign of a high level of evolution. But we are not sufficiently aware of what, in reality, is sensed. The attention of the human mind is constantly identified with thoughts and perception, most often spent in a state of day dreaming. The sense of Me is functioning merely as a self-conscious mechanism within the mind, so it can become self-attentive to its own psychological-mental activity. The excessive identification with the Me in motion, and the unawakened awareness of Me in itself, are the symptoms of what is called ignorance.

Ignorance simply means a lack of wholeness. The sense of being of most is fragmented and distorted. There is no center of presence. Each thought and emotion creates a separate Me, a mirage without substance. Complete identification with the psychological stream does not allow one to experience any sense of clear identity, any real connection with one's own self. One is deprived of basic peace and sanity. Ignorance is a state of deep and unconscious suffering.

Transcending Ignorance

Every human being experiences the sense of Me, a sense of the subject behind thoughts and feelings. In the dream state, the sense of Me is usually completely dispersed in the projections of the subconscious mind. In the dream, one experiences fears and joy, suffering and pleasure but rarely refers in a clear way to the sense of Me. In daily experiences, the sense of Me comes and goes, between periods of absorption in thought processes. The sense of Me, which is in reality the Soul herself, presents itself as a natural function of our consciousness.

Due to immaturity, Me is not appreciated and understood by the ignorant mind. Our identification with what is thought and felt does not allow us to bring the light of our attention to Me itself. However, when the attention turns back toward the very subject, one automatically steps back from the mind to the experience of Me. The lack of understanding of what, in reality Me is, brings us to the point of full identification with the substitute false identity, the ego-image. The ability to create the ego-image is certainly a natural function of human consciousness. But the moment we identify this ego-image with Me, with "what I am," the next layer of ignorance is added. The sense of Me is available to all normal human beings, but due to excessive identification with the mind, we hardly register its very presence. Bringing back the attention that is dispersed in thinking activity to the sense of Me is the only way to transcend the bondage of the unconscious, mechanical mind.

What are the essential qualities of this Me, which is the very primal experience of myself? They are Feeling, Attention, Being and Intelligence. We can experience them separately, but ultimately they are one, and need to be integrated. The original feeling-flavor of Me comes from the Heart. The Attention quality, the essence of its awareness, is born in the third eye center. The Being aspect represents the energetic presence of our very existence which has its root in the belly. Intelligence is the faculty of recognition, knowing and becoming aware.

To transcend the unconscious mind, one must develop the Attention aspect of Me that is nothing but the direct, bare self-conscious recognition of oneself. When one pulls the attention from the place of being immersed in thinking back to oneself, one shifts to the state of self-attention. This experience is instantaneous, direct and has the flavor of the impersonal. In the process of cultivation, of bringing oneself constantly to the state of self-attention, gradually one arrives at the point of stabilization in this state, which is the goal of all seekers.

Attachment to the Attention aspect of Me however, can prevent one from getting in touch with the deeper aspect of Feeling. This is the prevailing tendency in traditions such as Buddhism, for example. Developing the center of attention is not the goal but the means to go deeper into oneself. One is not able truly to feel the Heart without the awakened awareness. The restless mind simply does not give us any chance to be present, and it is only through the Presence that our intelligence can enter the Heart.

Human consciousness is an evolution of Me. The

ignorant Me or the lower form of Me is the identification with the mind, when Me feels itself only in the context of psychological events. This is called the state of forgetfulness. The higher form in the evolution of Me is the state of Presence, in which the Me feels itself as the self-recognizing attention. Certainly there is an element of feeling which comes from the Soul. Even in the state of disidentification with feelings (an ideal in some spiritual schools) one still experiences the "minimum" of the Soul, without which one could not possibly exist as an alive being. In the next step of evolution, the Feeling aspect, that is the Heart, is embraced in the holistic experience of the Me. The Presence (aspect of Me) allows one to be free from the mind and to discover one's true identity within the Heart.

Me, in its essence, is the unity of awareness, feeling and intelligence that is directly experienced as "myself." When the being quality is added, Me for the first time experiences the I Am. To experience I Am, Me must to some extent, let go of the self-referral mechanism. Me and I Am are one and different at the same time. We could say that without Me there is no experience of I Am, and without I Am, Me is not experiencing itself fully. The I Am is the area of beingness that links Me with the universal I AM. The I Am contains the whole of Me and the Me is the experiencer of I Am. The awakening of the Presence allows Me to have a stable experience of itself for the first time. The awakening of the Heart takes Me to the experience of its Divine essence and beauty. Intelligence is the primal force of conscious evolution, without which there is no Me. And finally, the Being is the dimension in which Me can rest in the Beyond, in Existence itself. The I Am is the conscious meeting of Me with the Totality of Creation.

The Awakening of the I Am

There are three basic aspects of I Am-Attention, Feeling and Being. The I Am we refer to is not the state of Presence but the wholeness of Me, the complete and awakened Me. We will not speak here about the aspect of Intelligence that represents the more dynamic essence of Me. Our interest is to describe the very foundation of Me, the I Am. The attention is generated in the mind; the feeling has its root in the Heart; and the being aspect represents our relationship to that on which everything rests, the Absolute.

All human beings experience more or less the Feeling aspect of I Am as the most natural quality. We are not referring here to the experience of emotions, but to the direct and intimate feeling of oneself, such as in sadness or loneliness. These feelings do not always refer to the pure experience of I Am, for they are most often tainted by the play of ego-images and various circumstances. However, they do refer to the sense of Me and are recognized as such. Because the feeling of Me is born in the Heart, it is only in the Heart that it can be experienced fully and directly.

The reason that most people are not aware of Me in itself, is their low level of consciousness and intelligence. The recognition and awareness comes from the mind, but because the mind is controlled by the mechanical and unconscious thinking process, it cannot be used as a tool of awakening. In order to recognize the I Am, one must transcend the unconscious mind so that the energy of awareness can be directed to the very subject, to the root of Me, to within. That which transcends the mind is the aspect of I Am called Attention. Attention is the present and conscious quality of our mind. It is that which is attentive to thoughts, feelings and surroundings. It goes beyond daydreaming and allows us to be aware within the thinking process. It is only this attention that makes us conscious and present, nothing else.

Because, as we mentioned, nothing but the attention can liberate us from the unconscious and mechanical mind, the foundation of all real spiritual disciplines is the cultivation of this attention. The essence of this cultivation is to bring the attention to the point in which it refers to itself and becomes aware of itself. At this stage we could, for example, use the thought "here and now," as a focal point of concentration. One must repeat this thought like a mantra, being fully conscious, attentive and present to it. In this exercise one experiences the presence of attention as directed toward the thought. After contemplating it for a time, one is asked to discern, "what is that which is aware of our mantra?" "What is this attention behind the thought here and now?" One learns how to turn the focus of attention to the attention itself. Then one is able to experience this attention in itself, as separated from mental objects. It is here that the Presence is born. The Presence, Pure Awareness or Witnessing Consciousness are names given to the Attention aspect of the I Am. Continuing the practice, one learns to retain the state of Presence in meditation as well as in activity.

The Being aspect of I Am can be experienced only in the vertical reality of the Now. We speak about that which allows us to be motionless and still within the movement of time and the elements. Attention, when it is attentive to itself, instantaneously steps out of the mind into the dimension of the Now. This attention in itself is called "Presence." The Presence anchors us into the Now and gives us roots which reach the timeless. The act of attention freezes the flow of time, but unless it is retained, it does not have the quality of Being. The experience of Being can occur only if the stillness of attention, that is Presence, has continuity within the flow of time. The continuity of stillness, of rest, of effortless abiding within the movement of time is what we call "Being."

Even when attention becomes aware of itself only for a split second, the quality of Being is present in this short moment. In meditation or rest, when the Presence naturally drops into itself and becomes absorbed, the Being quality goes deeper, and one rests more and more within the Now. In meditation, when the state of Presence is clearly experienced, one relaxes and lets the energy drop toward the belly. The Being aspect is experienced in "non-doing" or "just sitting," when one simply rests in the whole experience.

The essence of spiritual discipline is the cultivation of the Attention aspect of I Am until it is integrated in itself, giving rise to the state of Presence. Next is the process of maturation and adjustment, in which Presence becomes more and more integrated within our Being. This is the process of transmutation of energy and growth of intelligence and sensitivity. This leads the seeker to the final stabilization in the state of Presence.

Stabilization means that the state is constant; its energetic and self-conscious aspect is continuously being experienced. The state of Presence is always a mixture of Attention and the Being quality. There is always a play of several aspects that constitute this state. There is the natural energetic presence-awareness of the state.

There is a simultaneous element of *becoming* conscious of the state. And there is an aspect of Being that allows the state to be, letting go and dropping the energy of consciousness to its own law of gravity, apart from the personal will. All of this constitutes the dynamic reality of the Presence.

The Feeling aspect is always a part of the sense of Me, and no wonder that it is somehow constantly present, even in the process of cultivating the aspects of Attention and Being. We can say that any experience is a mixture of feeling, awareness and intelligence. After awakening to the fullness of I Am, all these aspects are integrated and balanced.

Although Feeling is always present, we experience it only minimally when focusing on the Attention or Being aspect exclusively (as in Zen, for example). We can focus more on the Being aspect, sitting often in absorption, without developing awareness and clarity. Or we can choose only the Attention aspect, which crystallizes the will and prevents us from being able to simply let go and relax. On the other hand, it is possible to cultivate the Feeling aspect alone, without developing the Attention and Being qualities. This is, in fact, the most popular focus in most spiritual paths that focus on the experience of love and devotion.

When the unconscious mind is transcended and the Presence awakened, one can go deeper into the Feeling aspect of the Heart. When Attention has continuity one not only feels the Heart but is actually present within the Heart. To be present within the Heart is to reach the essence of Me. The I Am, though it embraces our whole being, has its roots in the Heart, and it is the Heart that is the center of the I Am. The unity of clear Awareness, Being and Heart is what the complete I Am is.

It is only the Beyond, however, that allows the I Am

to fully realize itself. There are two fundamental dimensions of the Beyond, the Absolute and the Creator. Together they constitute the universal I AM. Thanks to the Absolute, one can realize the quality of Pure Rest. The Beloved, on the other hand, allows us to realize our Divinity. Only resting in the Beyond is the I Am complete.

If the Absolute State is not reached, the Being quality of the I Am is not fully realized. The Being quality represents that which rests upon the Absolute, that which is upon the Absolute. The absolute Now being reflected in the purity of I Am, is called Pure Beingness. It is very interesting that even when I Am is realized, though it is fully present, unless the Absolute is reached, the Being aspect of the I Am is not complete. The unmanifested, in a mysterious way, embraces the wholeness of I Am. The evolution toward the complete apperception of I Am takes place within this I Am. However, for it to be seen fully, I Am must reach the condition of Pure Rest within the Unborn. It is possible also for the Absolute to be realized and the I Am to still lack completeness, because the other aspects are not fully realized (Awareness or the Heart). The evolution of I Am happens through I Am and within I Am. Nevertheless, it is the Absolute, the principle prior to I Am, which allows I Am to apperceive itself as it is.

The experience of Beingness is also incomplete until the depth of the Heart is awakened. Beingness without the Heart represents the pure energy of rest. The Heart brings the fullness and beauty of the Divine. It is the Creator herself that is met in one's Heart. The Heart, though it is felt in our human form, is rooted in the Beyond. It is the dimension of the Beloved. Only in deep connection with the Creator can the I Am be finally fulfilled.

Verification of Attainment:
The Seeker's Goal

One of the most critical and sensitive moment in the spiritual journey is the verification of one's attainment. What is the criteria through which one can know that one has arrived and completed the inner work? Certainly, it is only our own intelligence and comparison with the descriptions given by the well-established spiritual traditions. There is no other way. The intelligence of a seeker must be supported by the wisdom of those who have already completed their path, in order to give rise to an accurate interpretation of what has been attained. The purpose of this book then, has been to give a precise description of the inner reality, free from spiritual superstitions and projections. In this attempt, we must bring to light some incorrect conclusions present in teachings from the past, in order to develop clarity and understanding, so the truth can be seen precisely as it is. On the other side, we need to expose the thick veil of superstitions and naíve projections created by the collective consciousness of the seekers themselves.

There are two major points that must be clarified. First is the quality, nature and subtle characteristics of the inner states. The second extremely important point is the full understanding of the rich and complex relationship and co-existence of the inner state and the very "Me," who is the seeker, experiencer, interpreter and enjoyer of all. This book has been evolving around these issues, and now we will try to put the pieces together. We will look at these matters from the view point of various potential pitfalls that may prevent the seeker from completely trusting in his/her attainment.

Verification of attainment is very important, for unless we know fully that we have arrived, we cannot evolve further. Realization of the inner is not the only goal of our journey. There is much more. To evolve further, we need to transcend the inner states and drop the practice. We can do this only if we know fully that the inner has been completed. If the seeker compares himself/herself with the master, there will always be a feeling of not yet having arrived. The reason may not be attainment of Enlightenment itself, but may be the age of the master, the maturity of his evolution in the inner state, and the energy of love and devotion of the disciples that surround him. We will summarize the inner states and their relationship to the personal self, in order to accurately assess our spiritual attainment.

I. A SUMMARY OF THE CHARACTERISTICS OF THE INNER STATES

The State of Presence

The realization and stabilization in the State of Presence, the I Am, is the major attainment for every true seeker. This attainment is not easy, and usually requires some years of cultivation and the presence of a Realized master. How do we know that we have attained this goal? It is quite simple. When the I Am is awakened and stabilized, there is a recognition of its constant presence at the background of our personality, no matter what we do. However, we may doubt that we have attained this state if we compare it with the descriptions given by the past spiritual traditions. Why is this? Because they suggest that this state has the quality of a stable and unchanging experience. As we know, the available teachings do not differentiate between the I Am and the Absolute State. The state of Presence, by its nature, fluctuates. Though it is constantly present, it is not absolutely motionless within itself. Its flavor and taste change depending on the situation and the well being of our psyche. It is constantly conscious but affected by the quality of our energy and our feelings.

To reach the I Am and to stabilize in it is a very high attainment on the spiritual path. But we may doubt that it is the "real" state when we notice that it is not absolutely free from the movement of energy. The very fact that there are different stages of absorption or samadhi shows us that there is change and movement within the state. This is the nature of the I Am consciousness. We must understand this clearly and accept it fully. Reaching this state is a sign of a highly evolved consciousness. Finally we have a refuge within our own Self from the tyranny of the mind, and we can rest in our own center.

The Absolute State
Because of its unchanging qualities, it is fairly easy to verify the attainment of the Absolute State with one's own intelligence. However, complete stability and the constant recognition of the Absolute takes place only after the integration process. After stabilization, one is directly linked with the state and can rest in it whenever one desires, but still there is a difference of feeling between resting in the Absolute and not resting. Before final integration with the Absolute, one may still experience the subtle movement of the Presence that

drops to the state of Pure Rest and moves out of it. Although the Absolute State after stabilization is constant, the recognition of it is not. It needs time to adjust, until the whole energy of Being is in full alignment with the condition of Pure Rest. It is important to see that although the state of Pure Rest is present, consciousness by its very nature still has certain tendencies to fluctuate. One experiences different qualities of consciousness, simultaneously abiding prior to it.

II. A SUMMARY OF THE RELATIONSHIP BETWEEN ENLIGHTENMENT AND ME

Doubtlessly, the understanding of what Me is and its relationship to the inner states is tremendously important in the art of verifying our attainment. Past spiritual traditions do not bring clarity to this issue. For this reason we need to speak about these matters carefully and precisely, deconditioning ourselves from wrong views that already have taken root in the collective consciousness. There are two major schools of thought, regarding the effect of Enlightenment on the situation of an individual. One speaks about the complete elimination of the sense of Me and disidentification with the personal self. The second assumes that Enlightenment gives to the individual special powers and abilities. Both approaches are extreme, indicating lack of a balanced perception of reality.

* Enlightenment does not annihilate the Me, neither is Me merely an "object," the "witnessed." The Me co-exists with the inner state. Apart from being *that* which allows the recognition of the state to happen, Me at the same time relates to this very state. The

inner state is a foundation upon which Me rests. However, the presence of Me is valid in itself, fulfilling its desires and evolving in its own dimension.

* Enlightenment has nothing to do with desirelesness. The inner state certainly has no desires, but the Soul who experiences it, in order to exist, must "desire." From the perspective of the inner state, it is irrelevant whether Me desires or not—the inner state simply *is* present. The idea that in order to reach Self-realization one has to eliminate desires, is very harmful and pulls seekers more deeply into ignorance. This is called spiritual ignorance.

* Enlightenment does not take away the experience of suffering, particularly as the Buddhists imagine. Suffering pertains to Me, and because Me does not magically disappear after the awakening of the inner state, in the same way, suffering continues to be a part of our reality.

* Enlightenment does not transform the personality automatically. It does not magically transform one's thinking, speech and action into pure positivity and compassion. The state of inner silence and stillness certainly has a strong impact on our personality, but it is not sufficient to fully cleanse the psyche. It is possible that after Enlightenment, one's Me may still be very unevolved or even psychotic. The evolution of Me runs <u>parallel</u> to the evolution toward inner states. The transformation of the Me is not a linear outcome of reaching any particular state. The deepest power of transformation comes from the opening of the Heart. The combination of the Absolute Rest and an open Heart allows the process of transformation and purification of Me to begin. This takes many years.

* Enlightenment to the inner state is not necessarily directly connected with the opening of the Heart. It

is possible to have an open Heart without Enlightenment and vice versa. For this reason evolution does not stop after Enlightenment. We could say the opposite: after reaching the inner states, the evolution at last can truly begin. Why? Because one has enough disidentification and inner-space to allow the reconstruction of the mind to take place.

* Enlightenment has nothing to do with acquiring powers and being charismatic. The collective projections from the master-disciple environments give the image of the Enlightened State as having a supernatural effect on the one who has reached it. Self-realization has nothing to do with special powers or a halo around the head. It is truly more related to the feeling of being ordinary in its profound sense. The descriptions of Saints and Masters given in books and scriptures, coupled with one's own natural dream of having miraculous powers, have for thousands of years conditioned humanity in the belief that supernatural powers are the very proof of attainment.

* The Enlightened One is not always perfectly aware and able to respond immediately to any challenge "without thinking." Enlightenment is not about being a Marital Arts master or a Samurai. The perfect alertness to the outer is not enough to bring one to the inner state; neither does being fully present in the inner state affect the quality of being attentive to the outer. Why is this? For the simple reason that totally different aspects of consciousness are responsible for awareness of the inner and the outer. Ultimately, the knowing of the inner has nothing to do with the personal will; it is unconditional.

* Enlightenment is not the attainment of "not-thinking." The Enlightened State is beyond thinking and non-

thinking. **Its very presence** transcends the mind. The attempt to **comple**tely eliminate thinking is an absolute **mistake and** against nature—it is not different from cutting off one's hands and legs. Thinking is part of the multidimensional wholeness of Me, therefore thinking cannot be discarded.

* Enlightenment does not necessarily bring awareness to the sleep state. Many seekers unquestioningly adopt the belief in the necessity of becoming aware of the inner state in the Sleep State. It is fine for the older masters who have completed their personal growth. In the case of young people, bringing awareness to the Sleep State is very unhealthy. It hinders the natural process of self-healing and the release of the subconscious mind in the dream state. The decision as to whether awareness is present in sleep or not belongs to the Absolute itself. For those who have shifted to the Absolute State, there is no longer will operating as far as "being within" is concerned. If we look more deeply into this idea of being aware in sleep or controlling the Dream State, what we find is fear. Many even fear that they will not be aware in the moment of death. It is madness.

Can Enlightenment be Lost?

As we know, the basic purpose of our practice is to stabilize in the inner state, whether it is the Presence or the Absolute. When one is stabilized, the need for practice is over, for the state is permanently and unconditionally present. However, our relationship with the state always has a dynamic quality. When the inner state is attained it is not yet all over. We must ask, who is Enlightened? Who is experiencing the inner state? The inner state is not all there is to Me. Me exists to be fulfilled in its own dimension, and not exclusively to enjoy the inner state. After stabilization the energetic presence of the Enlightened state cannot be lost, but the Me can lose its *Enlightened relation* to the state. It is possible for Me to lose all interest in the state, being pulled by the negativity of the mind. Stabilization in the inner state is like coming out of the womb: one cannot return. However, though Enlightenment cannot be lost, the Enlightened understanding and appreciation of it can be. For true Enlightenment encompasses the presence of the inner state and the wholeness of intelligence which recognizes it.

*****

* Only if we are able to see through the veil of projections and conditionings do we have the chance to encounter the true reality of our attainment. For the first time we see not "how it should be," but how it <u>is</u>. The verification of our attainment is a great challenge, for we must face the illusion of our projections, as well as of our relationship with the Enlightened state.
* The elimination of the past is not the transforming power of awakening, but the "adding" of our Enlightened state to our past, which brings about the enlightened Now, a transformed Now, Here and Now. That is why it is more precise to say that after the attainment of the Enlightened state one still experiences karma, but a "transformed" karma. This transformation is the very presence of the Enlightened state.
* Hence, with the gradual acceptance of the reality of one's attainment, and seeing through one's myths regarding Enlightenment, one can undertake the sensitive task of the final verification. After examining

one's state sincerely and precisely with a complete understanding of all of its inner and outer elements, it is possible for one to discover that indeed, one is established in that Exalted state. One has attained the Truth of Enlightenment.

The Last Word . . . . .

From the womb of Creation, two Souls were born to the ancient journey of time, gathering, piece by piece, the only Divine mirror that could reflect their secret faces, their mystery.

They saw in this mirror the very spirit, the very intelligence that mapped their very journey and designed their particular suffering and longing; and the very Heart of Grace. In this seeing, their primordial purity, prior to gathering the dust of time was revealed—they were washed clean from the paradox of Being and Becoming, from the Here and the Now.

In the divine purification of their existence in time, all was dissolved back into the timeless ether, except one Jewel: their first and ultimate meeting with the Beyond. This supreme encounter remains eternally in the molecules of Universal Consciousness, for only through the power of this encounter could they return again to the original womb.

It was in this womb that the Revelation of the Supreme Understanding reached their Heart—from this very womb they were touched by the faceless hands that transmitted to them, one by one, the existential pieces of their Divine mirror. It was here that their journey in the timedimension surrendered itself to their evolution in timelessness. Here, their will exhausted itself, giving birth to the transparency, their inherent purity.

In that transparent purity, that which needed to be

said was said to them. That which was being heard, was written. And that which was written, manifested the Revelation of Supreme Understanding.

Two Souls from the time-dimension entered the timeless womb of Creation, and gave birth to an understanding beyond their earthly imagination...

That which gave birth to them in the beginning, gave birth to them in the end.

That which gave birth to them in the end, gave birth to the Supreme Understanding. And that which gave birth to the Supreme Understanding, is giving birth to you Now. In Peace, in Love and in Grace.